Other books by Stansfield Turner

Secrecy and Democracy—The CIA in Transition

Terrorism and Democracy

Caging the Genies

Caging the Genies

A Workable Solution for Nuclear, Chemical, and Biological Weapons

Stansfield Turner

Westview Press
A Member of the Perseus Books Group

Copyright © 1999 by Westview Press, A Member of the Perseus Books Group

Published in 1999 in the United States of America by Westview Press, 5500 Central Avenue, Boulder,
Colorado 80301-2877, and in the United Kingdom by Westview Press, 12 Hid's Copse Road, Cumnor
Hill, Oxford OX2 9JJ

Library of Congress Cataloging-in-Publication Data
Turner, Stansfield, 1923–
    Caging the genies : a workable solution for nuclear, chemical, and
biological weapons / Stansfield Turner. — 2nd ed.
        p.   cm.
    Includes bibliographical references and index.
    ISBN 0-8133-6677-1
    1. Weapons of mass destruction.   2. Arms control.   3. No first use
(Nuclear strategy).   4. Security, International.   I. Turner,
Stansfield, 1923–   Caging the nuclear genie.   II. Title.
U793.T87   1999
327.1'747—dc21
                                                                    99-13854
                                                                        CIP

The paper used in this publication meets the requirements of the American National Standard for
Permanence of Paper for Printed Library Materials Z39.48-1984.

10   9   8   7   6   5   4   3   2   1

In memory of my parents, Wilhelmina and Oliver,
whose gift of example and whose love and encouragement
gave me the confidence always to reach a little higher;
and to my brother Twain, whose shortness of life forced me
to search for deeper meaning in my own

CONTENTS

ACKNOWLEDGMENTS

Since the original publication of this book in September 1997, concern for the threat that biological and chemical weapons pose has grown. This second edition of *Caging the Nuclear Genie*, retitled *Caging the Genies: A Workable Solution for Nuclear, Chemical, and Biological Weapons*, addresses that concern. Chemical and biological weapons are similar enough to nuclear weapons that the three are commonly grouped in a single category: weapons of mass destruction. I found, then, in laying out the problems these weapons pose and the solutions applicable to them, that the structure for dealing with nuclear weapons was quite adequate for dealing with the others also. Thus, analyses of chemical and biological weapons are integrated throughout the text as appropriate.

The original book would not have been feasible without generous grants from the Carnegie Corporation of New York. In addition to being most grateful for that support, I am appreciative of the advice and encouragement there of David Speedie and the late McGeorge Bundy. "Mac's" perceptive work in the area of nuclear weapons was a constant guide and benchmark.

I am also very grateful to the W. Alton Jones Foundation for the grant that gave this project its initial momentum and to George Perkovich for his helpful advice from beginning to end.

This second edition was made possible by The Fourth Freedom Foundation, which provided a generous grant in support of it.

The Norwegian Nobel Institute of Peace kindly provided me a Senior Research Fellowship and a stimulating environment in which to pursue the original effort for six months. They assembled a diverse group to critique the work in progress, including Christoph Bertram of Hamburg and

Pavel Baeev of Moscow. Geir Lundestad and Odd Arne Westad of the Nobel Institute offered helpful comments throughout my stay in Oslo.

John Chipman and Rose Gottemoeller of the International Institute of Strategic Studies in London were generous in bringing together a seminar to review an extended outline of the book. That group included some of the most prominent thinkers in this area, including Sir Michael Howard and Lawrence Freedman. I am most grateful to all of them for taking so much of their time.

The Peace Research Institute of Oslo also was kind in organizing a helpful seminar discussion that included Magne Barthe, Nils Petter Gleditsch, and Robert Bathurst.

I have been fortunate in having had assistance with research from a number of individuals during a span of four years. Hanno Kirk, Howard Diamond, Matt Didaleusky, and Jason Pate were able to devote the most time to it and were invaluable both for the facts they uncovered and the advice they proffered. Kurt Wendt, Zach Patrick, Milton Leitenberg, Garrett Ogden, Alex Slesar, and Peter Copeland also provided wonderful support. For this second edition of the book, Jason Pate and Hanno Kirk continued to provide major help and were joined by Erik Leklem, whose help was also most valuable.

Many individuals were kind enough to meet with me and offer suggestions: Robert McNamara, Bill Perry, and Dick Cheney, former secretaries of defense; Admiral Henry Chiles, then commander in chief of the U.S. Strategic Command; General Lee Butler, former commander in chief of the U.S. Strategic Command; Michael Nacht, Al Lieberman, and Fred Nyland of the U.S. Arms Control and Disarmament Agency; Janne Nolan, John Steinbrunner, Bill Kauffman, and Bruce Blair of the Brookings Institution; Roger Molander, Bruno Augenstein, and Jim Digby of the RAND Corporation; Robert Piacesi and Paul Garvin of G&P Associates, Inc.; Sergei Rogov of the Institute of the USA and Canada Studies in Moscow; James Jacobs of the Federal Emergency Management Agency; Steve Hadley, formerly of the Department of Defense; Bruce Russett and Gaddis Smith of Yale University; Father Brian Hehir of Harvard University; Brigadier Generals Jim Mathers and Lance Lord and Colonels Bob Kehler and Jack Byrnes of the U.S. Space Command; Major General Gary Curtin and Brigadier General Thomas Neary of the U.S. Strategic Command; Admiral Elmo Zumwalt, former chief of naval operations; Fred Ikle, Zbigniew Brzezinski, and Michael Mazaar of the Center for Strategic and International Studies; Harald Müller of the Peace Research Institute, Frankfurt; Spurgeon Keeny of the Arms Control Association; George Questor, Mancur Olson, Thomas Schelling, Ivo Daalder, and Steve Fetter of the University of Maryland; Colonel Ronald Williams of the Defense Special Weapons Agency; and Andrew Marshall and Frank Miller of the U.S. Department of Defense. I am particularly indebted to former President Jimmy Carter not only for his spending time to give me very important advice on the thrust of the book but also for reading and commenting on portions of it.

Ted Postol of MIT not only tutored me on the lethality of nuclear weapons but also did numerous calculations at my request. Kosta Tsipis, also of MIT, provided invaluable advice as to my use of the study he directed, "Nuclear Crash—The U.S. Economy After Small Nuclear Attacks."

I imposed upon many friends to read and make suggestions on various drafts. Their assistance in this was invaluable, both because they agreed and because they disagreed: Robert Monroe, Donald Rivkin, John Keeley, John Kieley, Ken Pollack, John Lewis Gaddis, Louis Halle, Robert O'Connell, John Rhinelander, Alton Frye, Eliot Cohen, Forrest Morgan, David Bradley, Richard Harza, Jeffrey Zink, Ove and Sjur Tjelta, George Thibault, Nordau Goodman, Stevan Dedijer, Mike Pocalyko, John Holdren, David Tall, Alvin Weinberg, Frank Tatum, Felix Moos, Staser Holcomb, Steve Nichalson, Alan Cranston, Charles Battaglia, David Rosenberg, Winn Price, William Karzas, Paul Grimes, Roger Ingle, Lynn Eden, and John Opel. This outpouring of support for finding ways to grapple with the vexing issues that nuclear weapons present has overwhelmed me. Having been shameless in asking for such assistance, I apologize if I have inadvertently overlooked someone upon whom I imposed.

Fran Burwell and Andrea White of the Center for International and Security Studies at Maryland rendered wonderful assistance and advice in administering the grants.

My assistant, Patricia Moynihan, had been through this process with me on two previous books and was just as wonderfully patient, exacting, and efficient with both the first edition and this one.

My wife, Eli Karin Turner, was not only my constant adviser and supporter but also my editor until the manuscripts were turned over to the publisher. Her ability to unravel my syntax in a language that is not her native one is superb.

None of the supporting individuals or foundations, of course, bears any responsibility for or necessarily endorses the content of the book.

Stansfield Turner

ACRONYMS

ΛBM	antiballistic missile
ADMs	atomic demolition munitions
AG	Australia Group
BWC	Biological Weapons Convention
CTBT	Comprehensive Test Ban Treaty
CTR	Cooperative Threat Reduction Program
CWC	Chemical Weapons Convention
EMP	electromagnetic pulse
FBI	Federal Bureau of Investigation
FEMA	Federal Emergency Management Agency
GDP	gross domestic product
GNP	gross national product
IAEA	International Atomic Energy Agency
ICBMs	intercontinental ballistic missiles
ISTC	International Science and Technology Center
KT	kilotons (thousands of tonnes)
MIT	Massachusetts Institute of Technology
MT	megatonnes (millions of tonnes)
MTCR	Missile Technology Control Regime
NATO	North Atlantic Treaty Organization
NFU	Treaty of No First-Use
NPR	Nuclear Posture Review
NPT	Nuclear Non-Proliferation Treaty
NSC	National Security Council
OTA	Office of Technology Assessment
SAC	Strategic Air Command
SALT II	Strategic Arms Limitation Treaty II
SDI	Strategic Defense Initiative

SIOP   Single Integrated Operational Plan
SLBMs   submarine-launched ballistic missiles
SLCMs   sea-launched cruise missiles
SSBN   strategic ballistic missile submarine
SSNs   attack submarines
StratCom Strategic Command
UN   United Nations

Caging the Genies

INTRODUCTION

O<small>N THE MORNING OF</small> F<small>EBRUARY</small> 26, 1993, a yellow Ford Econoline van parked on the second level of the public garage underneath the World Trade Center in New York City's lower Manhattan. At 12:18 P.M. there was a horrendous explosion that ripped through the garage and into the office buildings, killing six people and injuring more than 1,000. The twin towers, each 110 stories high, were shaken from their foundations to their tops, filled with smoke and without electricity. There was a crater about 120 feet in diameter and five stories deep where the bomb, estimated to be more than 1,000 pounds of high explosive, had detonated. The damage to the buildings was repaired sufficiently within twenty days for them to be reoccupied—but not so the damage to our American psyche. We abruptly became much more aware that our country is vulnerable to indiscriminate, unclaimed acts of terrorism.

Inevitably, there was speculation as to the consequences had it been a nuclear bomb. The A-bomb that the United States dropped on Hiroshima in August 1945 would have fit inside the Econoline van, and if one of the so-called rogue states—North Korea, Iran, Iraq, Syria, Libya, Sudan, and Afghanistan, for instance—or terrorists were to build a nuclear bomb, it would likely be a relatively simple, large one, much like the one employed at Hiroshima. That bomb released more than 10,000 times as much explosive power as the one in the van at the World Trade Center. Needless to say, had such a nuclear bomb been successfully placed and detonated in that building's garage, the consequences would have been terrifying. Within a fraction of a second of the explosion, intense light from hot, expanding gases could set fires in buildings up to a mile away. Depending on the bomb's location inside the garage, its detonation would vaporize or destroy major foundation supports of either one or both of the towers.

This would, within seconds, cause one or both of the massive buildings to slowly begin to topple. Everyone within a toppled tower probably would be killed. Within seconds of detonation, chunks of building debris carrying radioactive material from the bomb would shower surrounding streets thousands of feet away. In the next minutes and hours, smaller radioactive particles would be carried by the prevailing winds and fall to the ground, creating a highly lethal radioactive area of perhaps one-half to three-quarters of a mile in width and several miles in length downwind. Some fire fighters and emergency workers inside these areas, along with citizens, would die from radiation exposure as they fought fires or tried to come to the aid of the injured. The possibility of hundreds of thousands of deaths and injuries could not be ruled out.

Even more alarming is the thought that a rogue state or terrorist group would be able to steal or purchase a nuclear warhead from a Russian weapon. It, too, would fit inside a van, and experts estimate that with some borrowed or hired expertise it could be rigged to detonate. It would be twenty times more powerful than the Hiroshima bomb and would cause much higher levels of death and destruction, casting an unimaginable pall over our society.

Still another harrowing possibility is that the terrorists could have attacked the towers using chemical or biological agents along with the high explosive. In fact, the group considered packing the bomb with sodium cyanide, but there is no forensic evidence that any was actually used. Given that smoke from the explosion moved quickly as high as forty floors, it is likely that had the terrorists effectively employed sodium cyanide the gas would have killed many hundreds of people as they attempted to flee the catastrophe. At the least, rescue efforts would have been hampered for hours, limiting rescuers to those personnel equipped with protective suits and masks. The effects of the dispersal of biological agents by the explosion could have been more severe. Had the bomb been packed with five to ten pounds of anthrax spores, enough could have survived the explosion to send up a cloud that would lethally infect hundreds, if not thousands. Unprecedented decontamination efforts lasting weeks or months would have been necessary. Beyond such specific effects, a biological or chemical attack on the United States would have a traumatic psychological impact. We can sense as much today, in the growing public concern over the possibility of such weapons being used against our country or U.S. forces overseas. A major challenge of the post–Cold War era, then, is to prevent irresponsible actors from acquiring nuclear, biological, or chemical weapons and to deter their use by those who possess them. There are many courses we can pursue toward these objectives. Core to them all, however, is the example we set in our treatment of each of these types of weapons. Unless our own house is in order, we will not obtain the international cooperation needed to prevent materials and technologies for making such weapons from falling into the hands of irresponsible nations and terrorists. We, unfortunately, are not well positioned to elicit international cooperation.

On the nuclear side, we still possess some 15,000 nuclear warheads, many more than can be justified. We are also seen by many nonnuclear nations as reluctant to reduce that number. To begin with, our current target of 3,500 warheads is still far above what we need, and our plans for getting to that number will take until the end of 2007. Beyond this, our official policy is to employ loopholes in the current nuclear arms control agreement to maintain 10,000 nuclear warheads. The effect of 10,000 detonations similar to that at Hiroshima is unimaginable; yet two-thirds of the warheads we plan to keep are much more powerful. Thus, would-be proliferators must conclude that if we see such value in possessing these weapons they could well have equally legitimate reasons for possessing some also. We are not in a good position to tell them otherwise. Russia has half again as many nuclear warheads as the United States; there are numerous reports that they are not being guarded adequately; and Russia's plans for reducing numbers are no better than those of the United States.

With respect to biological weapons, the United States has taken a more positive position by unilaterally renouncing any use or even possession of them. In 1972 we signed and ratified an international agreement, the Biological Weapons Convention (BWC), to rid the world of these instruments. Where there is a shortcoming today is in balancing the need for an enforcement mechanism for the BWC against the concern of the American pharmaceutical industry over protection of proprietary information. On the Russian side, the picture is murkier. Russia has also signed and ratified the BWC, but there is evidence that biological warfare programs are being continued clandestinely.

With respect to chemical weapons, the United States in 1969 unilaterally declared it would never use them first and in 1993 signed the Chemical Weapons Convention (CWC), which prohibits the use, production, stockpiling, transfer, and acquisition of chemical weapons. The United States ratified the treaty in 1997. Ratification did not come easily, however, out of concerns both over the chemical industry's proprietary data and whether the CWC is verifiable. Russia also signed the CWC in 1993 and ratified it in 1997. Today the Russians profess that they cannot devote the necessary resources to destroy their existing stocks of these weapons by 2007 as stipulated in the CWC.

In short, even though there is a great deal of activity, neither Russia nor the United States is exercising decisive leadership with respect to nuclear, biological, and chemical weapons. Time is of the essence in correcting these situations. Every year that goes by increases the risk that rogue states and terrorists will achieve their ambitions for acquiring them. We now know firsthand how far Iraq had progressed toward a nuclear capability before its program was interrupted by its defeat in the Gulf War of 1991. And we know that before that war Iraq had already fielded a considerable capability for delivering chemical and possibly biological weapons. We know from intelligence reports that North Korea was on the brink of nuclear capability when we convinced it to stop its program, at least temporarily, in 1994. We were fortunate to be able to arrest these attempts at proliferation, and we cannot risk letting other rogues or terrorists get as close.

This, then, is the moment for the president of the United States and congressional leaders—Republicans and Democrats alike—to step forward: If only they could break with the routines of the Cold War, they could easily accelerate the nuclear arms reduction process and work more aggressively to eliminate biological and chemical weapons. Concurrently, they could help design and build an international regime to forestall any use of any of these so-called weapons of mass destruction. This book is dedicated to these momentous goals and suggests ways to move toward them without risking our nation's security. Indeed, it is difficult to conceive of any leaders in history leaving a more lasting mark or more meaningful service to humankind than seizing this opportunity to eliminate once and for all time the global threat of weapons of mass destruction. That would be the most important dividend of the end of the Cold War.

Part One

The Problem

1

THE SPELL CAST BY WEAPONS OF MASS DESTRUCTION

ONE AFTER ANOTHER THE JETS ROARED OFF the catapult and down the aircraft carrier's deck to be hurtled into the night sky. With only a few shielded lights about the ship, the sudden, bright-white glow of the afterburners as the pilots pushed throttles to maximum was an eerie sight. It was also an impressive scene of precision teamwork with lives constantly at stake.

I had witnessed carrier operations many times before, though my naval career had been in surface ships, not aviation. On this evening in September 1970, the flight operations had special meaning for me. I had just been promoted to rear admiral and had taken command of Task Group 60.2, the Navy's striking punch in the eastern Mediterranean Sea centered in this carrier, USS *Independence*. As I watched those aircraft taking off, I pondered my responsibilities for them. What would their specific missions be if war came? The next day I set out to find out.

I decided to start at the upper end of the Task Group's responsibilities—the possibility of nuclear war. I asked that a pilot with a nuclear mission and his bombardier brief me on what they were assigned to do if we were ordered to execute the nuclear war plan. A tall, strapping lieutenant in his late twenties and a handsome lieutenant (junior grade) a few years younger came through the door of my cabin, one carrying a targeting folder.

They began by explaining that their mission was but one of thousands in the Single Integrated Operational Plan (SIOP) for nuclear war. The SIOP included what not only our aircraft in *Independence* would do but also the Air Force's intercontinental ballistic missiles (ICBMs) and bombers, as well as the Navy's submarine-launched ballistic missiles (SLBMs) and aircraft from other carriers. The reason for having a SIOP, they noted, was to ensure that someone attacked every target the president selected and that the attacks did not interfere with one another. The pilot then went over the flight procedures he would use to protect his aircraft from the blinding flash and immense blast effects of the very detonation he and his bombardier were going to trigger. Impatiently, I asked, "But what are you going to attack?" Their target, the lieutenant said, was a railroad bridge spanning a river in Bulgaria.

Bulgaria! I found it incredible that anyone would believe any target in Bulgaria could be more than a tertiary concern if the SIOP were executed and a major nuclear war were raging across continents. Yet here were two young men prepared to risk their lives to drop a nuclear bomb on this bridge. They had their assignment and had to take it seriously. For my part, I had expected their target to be in the southern underbelly of the Soviet Union, perhaps the naval and bomber bases in the Crimea that were within range. It appeared to me this aircraft carrier had been assigned inconsequential targets because the United States had many more nuclear weapons than it needed.

For the sake of the flyers, I did my best to appear only modestly surprised. In feigning interest, I asked to look at the photograph of the bridge in the target folder they had brought along. The officers, a bit chagrined, pointed out that in the photo you could see where the railroad tracks stopped on either side of the river. The bridge, though, was too small to be visible! The aim point they had selected was the blank space in the river between the ends of the tracks.

About a year after this first exploration into nuclear targeting, I was on duty in the Pentagon. One of my responsibilities as chief of systems analysis for the Navy included analyzing the numbers and kinds of nuclear forces the Navy should have. One day I received an invitation to a briefing by the Air Force on the SIOP. I jumped at it. Nuclear war plans were normally shared with only a small group of officers who were more directly involved than I in nuclear matters. I hoped the briefing would shed some light on why we were bothering with a Bulgarian bridge.

On the appointed day, about fifty people gathered in a briefing room. The briefing officer had maps and charts that divided the SIOP's targets into several categories. He discussed whether the weapons assigned were ballistic missiles or aircraft bombs and whether they would be delivered by the Air Force or the Navy. As he went along it became clear that almost all of the targets he enumerated were military ones. Only at the very end did he discuss industrial and economic targets and the weapons allocated to them. Then I understood why so many of us had been invited to this briefing: We were being asked to persuade our superiors to support the acquisition of additional nuclear warheads in order to have enough to deal with industrial targets more comprehensively. I asked what our inventory of warheads was at that time. The answer was about 27,000: About 20 percent were intercontinental-range strategic warheads; about 80 percent were short-range tactical warheads. The 27,000 total, however, was down from about 32,500 a few years earlier. The argument was that we needed to go back up.

When I went to bed that evening, I had difficulty getting to sleep. I kept thinking, *That was the most frightening briefing I've ever heard!*

These two incidents—the review I had received onboard ship of one target in the SIOP and the briefing in the Pentagon on the overall SIOP—were the first seeds for this book.

COMMON SENSE TELLS US that 27,000 nuclear warheads, let alone the peak of 32,500, far exceeded any conceivable need the United States could possibly have had. How unrealistic were such numbers? It would take 55 billion aircraft bombs, each bomb containing 500 pounds of TNT, to unleash as much energy as 32,500 nuclear warheads.[1] To put this in perspective, each state in the union could be carpeted with 1 billion bombs with 5 billion to spare—something quite beyond imagination. To put it another way: The power of the 32,500 warheads would roughly equal 1 million Hiroshima-type bombs,[2] one of which destroyed almost all of the buildings within a twelve-square-mile area and killed 140,000 of the city's 350,000 people during the first five months after detonation.[3]

Of our maximum of 32,500 warheads, some were large and designed for intercontinental-range weapons to attack industrial or population targets or to destroy installations that were hardened against nuclear attack. Others were small (by nuclear standards; they were enormous by those of conventional weapons) and intended for short-range use on the battlefield. There have to be plans for utilizing each category, and those plans can be complex (e.g., if a large warhead arrived within about twenty minutes of an earlier one, the second might be neutralized by the debris thrown up by the first). With such large numbers of warheads and the variety of options for employing them, by the 1980s our nuclear war plan filled more than 1 million pages. General Lee Butler told me that when he took over command of the Strategic Air Command (SAC) in 1991 (in 1992 SAC became the Strategic Command, or StratCom, which Butler commanded until 1994), he began a month-long effort to review every aspect of the master war plan, including each of the 12,000-plus targets. One of his conclusions was that no single person on his staff had a grasp of all of the factors essential to creating a coherent nuclear war plan. Such complexity in nuclear war plans makes it almost impossible for anyone to be certain that directives from the president or the secretary of defense are actually reflected in them. Some experts have even asserted that declaratory policy changes made by presidents and secretaries have often resulted in few, if any, changes to the plans themselves. And given this million-page complexity, it has been difficult for presidents to appreciate fully what options they had or to be ready to inject new ones of their own during a crisis. Rather small changes could have such interlocking effects that it could take a year to insert them. For much of the nuclear era, presidents were effectively limited to a small number of options—all involving massive numbers of weapons.

It is almost incomprehensible that there was so little questioning of the merit of adding or subtracting warheads from a base of tens of thousands. How could anyone have been so concerned about the difference between 27,000 and 32,500 as to warrant the lobbying effort to which I had been subjected? It was not until the late 1980s that anyone in high authority addressed the issue of excess targets in our war plans head-on. Why did it take so long to do this? In part, intense secrecy made it difficult for decisionmakers to know just what was going on. Yet there have been thousands of officials in the executive branch and in Congress who were privy to an annual directive signed by the president specifying the number of nuclear warheads we would have for the next year. It should have been easy enough to recognize that 32,500 warheads was an unconscionably high number, regardless of the number the Soviets, later the Russians, possessed. In my view it was just too difficult for those officials to tear themselves away from the logic of conventional warfare, where it is always better to have more weapons than your opponent. And because the stakes seemed so high, the military planners grossly overestimated the allowance needed for possible faulty weapons, approximating two warheads for every target requiring one. And finally, from a psychological and emotional perspective, it seemed essential to national security planners that we stay ahead in the race for "superiority," as well as espouse the view that we could "win" even in a nuclear war. President Ronald Reagan's first secretary of defense, Caspar Weinberger, stated it clearly: "You show me a secretary of defense who is planning not to prevail in nuclear war, and I'll show you a secretary of defense who ought to be impeached."[4] This hyperbole reflected the fact that any political leader who did not profess that we should spend enough to win in nuclear war ran the danger of being called soft on communism. One analyst of this situation noted that "no administration has been able to disavow the prospect of emerging from a nuclear conflict with some kind of meaningful victory."[5]

What we did, then, was to make parity with the Soviets our minimum level of comfort. Accordingly, we kept ratcheting our number of weapons upward as they did theirs, in their own quest for at least parity. This situation was compounded by the fact that our stated objective has always been deterrence. Deterrence requires posing a threat of unacceptable damage in retaliation to any attack with nuclear weapons. As the opponent's nuclear arsenal increased, we felt ours had to also, lest our deterrent threat somehow diminish. Deterrence, however, is in the eye of the beholder. We just never asked why the Soviets, if they surpassed us in nuclear capability, would no longer feel deterred, even though we would still pose a threat of unacceptable retaliation.

The more nuclear weapons we had, the greater the risks we took in managing them. In contriving uses for nuclear weapons in war plans, planners came closer and closer to intellectual dishonesty. This way of thinking was set at the very beginning, when President Harry Truman directed that the first atom bomb be employed against a military target. The

Army Air Corps selected a military headquarters in Hiroshima. It may well have been an important military target, but it was also at the center of the city. Most of the 70,000 people who died immediately, and the additional 70,000 who died within the next few months, were not associated with that headquarters. It is easy to believe that the people who selected the target were hypocritical in pretending it was a military target, since most of the bomb's impact would be against nonmilitary installations and people. Still, although that must have been very clear to them, these planners were required to select a target that when destroyed would stun the Japanese into surrendering. Whatever their motives or consciences, those first nuclear targeteers were forced to face up to *the* moral dilemma of the nuclear era: how to take advantage of the vast power of these weapons without unwanted ancillary effects.

We had been quietly avoiding this dilemma with the firebombings of Dresden, Tokyo, and five other Japanese cities during the final six months of World War II.* After Hiroshima we could not avoid it. The further we have moved from World War II, the more public deference we have paid to morality in nuclear targeting. For more than thirty years our declaratory policy has been that we do not target cities. That, however, has not by any means solved matters. For instance, during the 1980s one of our war plans, which supposedly did not target cities, included fifteen nuclear detonations within ten miles of the Kremlin. Again, if this was not hypocrisy, it was an example of targeteers being caught between conflicting requirements: one to accomplish sufficient damage, the other to avoid cities. Because it fell to military planners to somehow resolve such antithetical demands, they have shaped our nuclear strategy—to the point where one must question whether the system has always been under adequate civilian control.

Dissembling in nuclear planning, though, has not been a matter for military planners alone. It reached to the highest levels of government in our doctrine to help defend our West European allies. This began in 1952 at a meeting of NATO's foreign ministers in Lisbon. NATO's military planners had assessed the Warsaw Pact's conventional military capabilities as being

---

*In total, our firebombings of Japanese cities killed more people than were killed immediately at both Hiroshima and Nagasaki. The directives to the targeting people in those cases, however, were for attacks on the cities themselves. There was no pretense at aiming at a military target. Hence, there was no issue of hypocrisy for the planners.

considerably superior to those of NATO. A goal was developed to field a total of ninety-six army divisions and associated forces, up from fewer than forty, many of which were skeletal. This was politically unacceptable to Europeans, as it appeared to set the stage for yet another large conventional war in Europe, and it was economically unacceptable on both sides of the Atlantic. Instead, NATO ministers accepted the nuclear superiority of the United States over the Soviet Union as establishing a general equilibrium. This was not a difficult concept for the United States to accept at the time, since there was relatively little risk. The Soviets had detonated their first nuclear device only three years before, built less than ten nuclear warheads compared with our approximately 450, and possessed very little potential for delivering them at intercontinental distances. Soviet nuclear capabilities grew over the next decade, however, appearing to offset our advantage to some extent. As Europeans looked for continued reassurance, it could only come from our being more specific as to just how our nuclear superiority would translate into the defense of Europe.

At a meeting of NATO's foreign and defense ministers in Athens in 1962, U.S. Secretary of Defense Robert S. McNamara suggested the possibility of halting "a Soviet advance into Western Europe by unilateral application of nuclear weapons on or near the battlefield."[6] This eased us into a pledge to initiate the use of nuclear weapons if necessary to repulse an invasion of Western Europe, even one by conventional forces of the Warsaw Pact. In 1967 NATO formally adopted nuclear response to conventional attack as its doctrine. For years, we assumed that disrupting the Warsaw Pact's rear echelons in Eastern Europe with tactical nuclear attacks would halt an advance. What we failed to address was whether the Soviets would respond in kind against NATO forces in Western Europe.

By the late 1960s, the Soviets had sufficient nuclear capabilities to do that. For Europe, with its limited geographical size, this could mean the loss of much of what was being defended. The Europeans sidestepped this dilemma by hypothesizing an American nuclear umbrella over all of Europe. If a conventional war being waged inside that umbrella went badly, they presumed we Americans would launch attacks with long-range nuclear weapons directly on the Soviet Union and outside the umbrella. That, of course, would open the United States to nuclear retaliation. Americans, in contrast, assumed we would employ short-range tactical nuclear weapons inside the umbrella. The retaliation would be on Western Europe. We made our intentions obvious by deploying some 7,000 tactical weapons to Europe. In 1979 Henry Kissinger pointed out, albeit after leaving the government, the unreasonableness of what the Europeans were expecting from us: "The European allies should not keep asking us to multiply strategic assurances that we cannot possibly mean, or if we do mean, we should not want to execute, because if we execute we risk the destruction of civilization."[7] Despite these irreconcilable positions, we and the Europeans continue to profess that under a policy of "extended deterrence" the United States will employ nuclear weapons to defend its allies against attacks by conventional forces, not just nuclear ones.

This bluff may well have contributed to deterring the Soviets from invading Western Europe. It certainly saved us and our allies the considerable costs of maintaining larger conventional forces to do the same. But this begs the question: Should we have placed the survival of Western Europe on the line in order to obtain those savings? It was not just an abstract risk we were taking. U.S. military forces in Europe were poised to use nuclear weapons the moment the fighting went against them, lest those weapons be overrun and without them we lose the war. General Bernard W. Rogers, the Supreme Allied Commander in Europe, said in 1984, "Because of our lack of sustainability—primarily ammunition, materials to replace losses on the battlefield, tanks, howitzers, trained manpower . . . I have to request the release of nuclear weapons fairly quickly after a conventional attack. And I'm talking in terms of days, not in terms of weeks or months."[8] The risk is that a military organization trained on a set of assumptions is all too prone to work from those assumptions in the event of a crisis.

But there is an even more hair-raising risk that we have taken and are continuing to take: the obsession with surprise nuclear attack. There is a thesis that assumes the Soviets (and even the Russians today) might try to disable our retaliatory capability through one swift blow and thus "win" a nuclear war. A 1954 study of the vulnerability of SAC bases conducted by RAND, a corporation formed and funded by the U.S. Air Force in early 1946 to do analytic work on military problems, concluded the Soviets could wipe out our entire SAC bomber force with a few dozen bombers in a surprise attack. It argued that the mere possession of nuclear weapons and delivery capability was not sufficient to deter such attack. If we were really to deter a surprise attack, the Soviets had to be persuaded that our strategic forces could survive an attack and then surmount any barriers to retaliation (such as active defenses or civil defense preparations) to deliver a crushing retaliatory blow. As it developed over time, this view held that any adverse changes in the balance of strategic forces or sudden techno-logical breakthroughs—perhaps in antimissile defenses or antisubmarine warfare—could upset a stable balance by creating what came to be known as a "window of vulnerability" to a surprise attack. Hence, no set number of nuclear forces could assure stable deterrence; rather, we always had to stay ahead of the Soviets quantitatively and qualitatively. Later, other worst case scenarios were added, including a sneak attack to destroy our command and control capability and a "decapitating attack" on our polit-ical leadership. All this was applying the deeply ingrained lessons of Pearl Harbor to the nuclear era erroneously because:

- The estimates of Soviet strength, technology, and force readiness were in error. A major point here is that the strategists at RAND, up to mid-1961, had to rely on inflated Air Force intelligence estimates. They did not have access to the super-sensitive intelligence sources. These included the U-2 and RB-70 spy planes, photographic reconnaissance satellites, signal intercepts, and agents on the ground. From 1961 on, these sources confirmed that the United States had never trailed in technology or numbers of strategic launch vehicles and that the United States, at worst, would have had several hours' warning as to secret Soviet preparations for a surprise attack (and more likely several days or weeks).
- The Soviets would have great difficulty executing a complicated simultaneous strategic strike at far-flung targets without giving us warning enough to retaliate. And after our first strategic ballistic missile submarine (SSBN) came on line in 1960, it became impossible for the Soviets to locate, let alone destroy, all of our retaliatory capacity in a surprise attack.
- The Soviets would pay an enormous price if a surprise attack failed and, having lost 20 million people in World War II, would hardly be indifferent to a death toll of equal magnitude in a nuclear exchange.

Nonetheless, we took substantial risks to ward off surprise attacks on our ICBMs and bombers by creating an elaborate warning system designed to enable us to launch a response between the time we detect an incoming attack and the time it actually impacts. The flight time of a ballistic missile from Russia to the United States is twenty-five to thirty minutes. Within two to seven minutes of launch we should have detected and identified any massive attack. There are elaborate procedures for crosschecking and evaluating the evidence while gathering senior military commanders and civilian officials on a conference telephone call. That could mean rousing people out of a sound sleep, interrupting meetings, locating those who are playing golf or shopping, and so on. There would be duty officers continuously in the command centers of the major military commands, the Pentagon, and the White House, but the probability of getting most of the principal officials on whom the president relies (e.g., the secretary of defense) on the phone within five to ten minutes is not high. Once these officials assembled, they would need some time to ask their own questions and to make their own evaluations before deciding to bring in the president. Scrambling a president summarily is not something that can be done cavalierly, especially if the commander in chief is engaged in some very public activity.

Thus, the president would be facing a very short deadline once brought into the debate. At least ten minutes, and more likely fifteen, would be needed to transmit an order to launch our weapons, to verify it, and to give the missiles and bombers time enough to launch and fly far enough away to avoid the effects of the incoming attack. That means there could be as little as three minutes, and at the very most eighteen, to assemble principals and for the president to make the most momentous decision in history (see Figure 1.1). It is irresponsible even to pretend we have the capability for making a decision of this import under these conditions—or that we would do so even if we could.

However, maintaining the pretense of being able to launch on warning has been an additional way of dissuading the Soviets, and now the Russians, from attempting a surprise attack. Yet that benefit must be weighed against the risk of keeping a large part of our nuclear force on constant hair-trigger alert. We have had thousands of false alarms of impending missile attacks on the United States, and a few could have spun out of control. One such incident took place on June 3, 1980. Zbigniew "Zbig" Brzezinski, President Jimmy Carter's assistant for national security affairs, was awakened at 2:26 A.M. by a phone call from Colonel William Odom, a

FIGURE 1.1   Best and Worst Cases for Firing Our ICBMs Under Attack from Russia

					Time of Impact
	0	2	12	20	30
Best Case	Time to Detect Attack	Time to Assemble Principals	Time to Decide	Time to Relay Orders and Fire Own Missiles	

				Time of Impact
	0	7	10	25
Worst Case	Time to Detect Attack	Time to Assemble Principals and Decide	Time to Relay Orders and Fire Own Missiles	

staff officer responsible for matters of nuclear readiness. Odom told him the warning system was predicting a nuclear attack of 220 missiles on the United States with the specific destination unknown. The alarm bells of nuclear alert were ringing, and the conference calls were under way. Shortly thereafter, Odom called back to say the warning indicators had changed to an all-out attack of 2,220 missiles. Bomber crews on alert were manning their aircraft and the Pacific Command's airborne command post had taken off. What flashed through Brzezinski's mind was that in less than thirty minutes it would be all over for him and most other Washingtonians. He was determined to ensure that the Soviet Union would be equally devastated but decided he had another minute before having to wake President Carter and confront him with a decision on whether to launch a counterattack immediately. Brzezinski asked Odom to give him one more update. Odom called again almost immediately to say that only one of our warning stations had reported the impending attack. The fact that no other station saw it indicated there was a computer error in the system. The crisis came and went in a matter of minutes.[9]

Still, the chances of our going to war on the basis of a false alarm have always been low. A president would see that releasing any number of nuclear weapons under such a circumstance would virtually guarantee that the United States would be subjected to a nuclear retaliatory strike, if indeed a preemptive one had not already been launched. The president would also understand it would be foolhardy to place anything like 100 percent confidence in any intelligence report about an impending attack. The consequences of being wrong could be so enormous that, I believe, any president would wait it out rather than make nuclear war certain.

Nuclear theorists think up and organize these elaborate procedures for firing nuclear weapons under pressure and for initiating nuclear war in the defense of allies. Since Nagasaki, there is no evidence that a president would have likely released nuclear weapons without an actual nuclear provocation. In short, there is a world of difference between concocting theories for the use of nuclear weapons and shouldering the responsibility of actually employing them. What would happen, though, if the system slipped from the president's control as a result of an accident or confusion during a crisis? If it fell into the hands of people we have trained in these theories, would they follow their training or be restrained by the weight of their decision? There is no way to know, but it is a sobering and dangerous aspect of our military posture, even today.

Another chilling aspect of that posture has been the physical dangers to which we have subjected the American people and others. The most glaring case was in 1961 when one of our B-52 strategic bombers broke up in flight over North Carolina. Two nuclear bombs of megaton size landed near Goldsboro. On one, five of the six safety switches failed. Only the last prevented detonation. Fortunately, the only untoward result was that some radioactive materials were spread over a small area.[10] This incident was one of eleven in which nuclear weapons were accidentally lost from aircraft in flight or were involved in accidents in aircraft during the 1960s, when we maintained strategic bombers on continuous airborne alert. We also have had accidents involving U.S. submarines with nuclear weapons embarked, none with any nuclear detonations.

The end of the Cold War has lulled us into believing we no longer need be concerned about the kinds of excesses and risks we have seen with respect to nuclear weapons. We no longer feel that a nuclear defense of Europe is necessary or that a surprise nuclear attack from Russia is at all likely. And we do not feel that a major nuclear confrontation, such as that experienced during the 1962 Cuban missile crisis, is at all probable. There are reasons, however, why such attitudes could prove to be negligently shortsighted.

First, we must recognize that there are a lot of nuclear warheads around. The bulk is in the United States, with more than 15,000, and Russia, with more than 22,000. China has about 500, France and Great Britain each something less than that.[11] In addition, in May 1998 India and Pakistan each tested nuclear weapons, confirming publicly their nuclear capability, something that had been in intelligence estimates for some time. India probably has the capability to produce about seventy-five weapons, Pakistan something less. Further, there is an assumption that Israel has 100-plus unacknowledged nuclear weapons immediately available.

Second, there is the overarching concern that as long as Russia has nuclear weapons numbering in the thousands the existence of our society in anything like its present form will be at risk. With consequences of that magnitude, we must remain positively engaged, no matter how slim we judge the probability of nuclear catastrophe to be. It is as basic as a homeowner's taking out insurance against the small chance the house will burn down. Even if all nuclear weapons were somehow to be destroyed, preventing the manufacture of new ones would require diligent attention. After all, the knowledge of how to make them cannot be erased. In short, we have a vitally important responsibility to future generations.

Third, we cannot predict where Russia will be in even a few years. It seems highly unlikely its economic base will permit it to be a confrontational adversary again for more than a decade. Unfortunately, that does not mean nuclear tensions could not regenerate. Today's Russian leaders are saying they cannot afford sufficient conventional military forces to match those of NATO and therefore must rely more on nuclear military power—the same tack we took in offering a nuclear umbrella to our NATO allies during the Cold War. Ultimately, Russia will again be a great power, and we do not want our nuclear relationship to return to being a tense one. We should do all we can to make that unlikely while we have the opportunity.

Fourth, whereas during the Cold War our dominant concern in the nuclear arena was a major nuclear war with the Soviet Union, we must now include a wider range of contingencies:

- There is the possibility that nuclear weapons will proliferate to rogue states and terrorists and that they will employ them deliberately.
- There is the risk of accidental, unauthorized, and mistaken use by the nuclear states. Today, the United States, Russia, China, Great

Britain, France, and Israel have all shown considerable caution in controlling their nuclear capabilities. India and Pakistan had been quite circumspect until their testing. We now must be concerned how well they will manage and control their newly acknowledged nuclear arsenals. Still, the risk of accident or error exists wherever there are nuclear weapons. The risk would be much greater if a state like Iraq or North Korea were able to procure a small nuclear arsenal. The emphasis on secrecy in such societies could conflict with establishing firm internal controls.

- Finally, there is the possibility of deliberate, rational use of nuclear weapons by existing nuclear powers. An Indian-Pakistani nuclear war could erupt; Israel could believe itself sufficiently endangered to resort to a nuclear defense; Russia could feel threatened by China or feel it is unable to meet problems created by neighbors with conventional forces; and China is a great uncertainty when we look to the future, although its current policy is no first-use of nuclear weapons.

Thus, with the end of the Cold War we must widen the focus of our efforts to deter nuclear catastrophe. Russia still remains the threat of greatest magnitude and, therefore, must remain our primary concern, even though lesser nuclear powers are more likely to use nuclear weapons deliberately. If we look ahead a quarter- or half-century, as we surely must in this analysis, it is not beyond imagination that world affairs could degenerate into occasional, limited use of nuclear weapons, including deliberate, accidental, or unauthorized employment of them. That would be a vastly different world in which to live, what with uninhabitable, pockmarked areas of contamination and the constant threat of instant, indiscriminate destruction hanging over populations. This is not necessarily the most likely nuclear direction, but it is a possible, if grim, prospect. Our policies on nuclear weapons must deal with Russia as well as all the other nuclear powers. In deciding how we deal with each, it should be evident that it would be a mere coincidence if the policies formulated in the crucible of the Cold War happened to be those best suited for the new world.

Most of our efforts during the Cold War to prevent the use of nuclear weapons—bilateral agreements between the United States and the Soviet Union—for the most part have been tortuously slow and of limited value thus far. The latest treaty, START II, promises to reduce intercontinental strategic nuclear warheads actually mated to delivery vehicles to 3,000–3,500 on each side (roughly one-third of what we possessed at the end of the Cold War) by the end of 2007. That helps by establishing that both major nuclear powers want a future with far fewer nuclear weapons, but 3,000–3,500 warheads would still constitute a grave threat to both societies. There is, then, no reason to worry less because of this numerically impressive goal. Moreover, the numbers are misleading. They do not include tactical nuclear warheads for short-range weapons and strategic warheads held in reserve and not mated to long-range delivery vehicles. Adding these in, the United States intends to maintain the 10,000 warheads noted earlier; the Russian figure is uncertain. At these levels each side could do so much damage that the reduction would be rendered meaningless: What does it matter whether we incinerate one another with 10,000 warheads or with 32,500?

There are other bilateral arms control agreements for which we have congratulated ourselves. Several limit the size of ballistic missiles and the number of warheads they carry. We have wanted to limit the number of Soviet warheads because of their supposed potential for surprise attacks. But we have such an overwhelming, assured capability to retaliate after any preemptive strike that this sort of limit is of minor import. Other steps we and the Russians have taken—without written agreement—are to remove some nuclear weapons from conditions of high alert and to shift the immediate targeting coordinates of others to spots in the oceans. These are commendable moves symbolically but largely cosmetic. Missiles on both sides can be reset to their wartime targets in a matter of seconds; and if a Russian missile were launched accidentally or illicitly, it would automatically switch back to its primary wartime target.[12]

Our second major approach to controlling nuclear weapons has been to pressure, cajole, and legally tie the hands of would-be proliferators and those abetting them—and we have been eminently successful here. South Africa voluntarily disposed of its five or six nuclear weapons; Ukraine, Belarus, and Kazakhstan returned to Russia all of the Soviet nuclear warheads that were in their territories when the USSR dissolved; we forestalled Iraqi and North Korean programs to develop nuclear weapons, at least for the time being (it remains unclear whether North Korea produced any weapons previously).

Still, the know-how for manufacturing nuclear weapons is openly available; more and more fissionable material is accumulating and generating a black market; Russian control over fissionable materials, nuclear technology, and even weapons themselves is increasingly seen as inadequate; and more countries are acquiring the sophisticated skills needed for manufacturing nuclear weapons as part of competing in the world marketplace. Yet assembling the materials and skills and actually manufacturing a nuclear weapon is not something that can be done in a garage by any mechanic. On balance, however, rogue states would likely be satisfied with a large, crude, Hiroshima-type nuclear weapon with lesser tolerances than ours; terrorists might even be content with nonexplosive, radioactive-contaminating devices. We would be naive to assume that if rogue states and terrorist groups have reason to believe acquiring nuclear weapons would be to their advantage they will not do so.

The incentives these parties see for proliferation today are: to gain leverage over traditional enemies; to deter such an enemy that has acquired them; to deter the United States from intervening with its superior conventional forces; and to terrorize the United States from spreading democracy and free enterprise around the world. Those incentives will persist as long as there is a perception that nuclear weapons can be employed usefully for such purposes. The United States is perpetuating that very perception by claiming it needs nuclear weapons to defend its allies against conventional military assaults. This undermines one of our major efforts against proliferation: the Nuclear Non-Proliferation Treaty (NPT),[13] which originally dates to 1968 and was renewed indefinitely in 1995 by 178 nations. Nations can, though, logically argue that they have vital interests that justify their acquiring nuclear weapons, even if it means abrogating the NPT. And they have an additional excuse in the provision of the NPT that requires the existing nuclear powers to do all they can to reduce the size of their nuclear arsenals with the objective of total elimination. If START II is fully implemented in 2007, we and the Russians will only be down to approximately the number of warheads we had at the time the NPT was signed. It is difficult to deny that progress on that front has been slow. The NPT, then, will be less of an assurance than we would like to believe until we and the Russians renounce claims that we have needs for lots of these weapons and actually make much greater reductions.

The Comprehensive Test Ban Treaty (CTBT), which bans any testing of nuclear weapons, is another achievement more of form than substance. It is supposed to be a barrier to proliferation, but Israel, Pakistan, and South Africa all developed their weapons without detectable testing (as did the United States with the weapon dropped on Hiroshima). Testing primarily provides confidence that a new, highly complex weapon will work. For rogue states and terrorists, moderate confidence in rather simple weapons that have not been tested will suffice. We would do well not to count too heavily on the CTBT to inhibit proliferation. And once a state breaks through the barriers to proliferation, there could be a snowball effect. For instance, should Iraq acquire these weapons, Iran would scramble to match its arch rival, and Saudi Arabia could feel exposed and want to follow suit. This is what happened in India, which acquired nuclear capability because it felt vulnerable to China's nuclear weapons; Pakistan then believed it had to match its neighbor. Should there be much additional proliferation, even responsible nations like Germany and Japan could feel pressures to become nuclear powers.

Unfortunately, the outlook for using the arms control process to make further progress in reducing the nuclear threat is not good. The best evidence of this is the agreements on arms control made by Presidents Bill Clinton and Boris Yeltsin at a March 1997 summit. In their efforts just to sustain momentum, they found it necessary to slow the arms control process, to complicate it, and to push difficult issues down the road. Specifically, they postponed full implementation of START II by five years; forced a second ratification of the revised START II by the U.S. Senate; and limited their ambition for a START III to 2,000–2,500 warheads each. What this tells us is that an already glacially slow process is confronting such problems that it is moving slower—and that we have no plan for getting across a threshold low enough to reduce meaningfully the nuclear danger under which we live.

Overcoming these impediments should be a topic of concern for every citizen. Even though most of us assume the problems of nuclear weapons are a secondary concern today, the amount of media coverage the issue receives is substantial and regular on topics like nuclear proliferation in general; the prospects for proliferation in Iraq and North Korea; our concern that Russia and China are selling materials that could contribute to proliferation; whether to maintain economic sanctions on Iran because of its nuclear ambitions; what we can do to help secure Russia's nuclear materials and weapons; the outlook for the NPT, the CTBT, and other treaties governing these weapons; intelligence on nuclear weapons; the

possibility of nuclear terrorism; ballistic missile defenses; future requirements for numbers and types of nuclear weapons and their delivery systems; and the contaminating aftereffects of past nuclear programs.

Yet despite such evidence of national concern, there is strong resistance
to changing our Cold War nuclear policies. A full-scale Nuclear Posture
Review (NPR) was conducted in the Pentagon in 1994. It concluded that
our current policies and programs were just about right, except that we
should use the looseness of START II to maintain the 10,000 warheads in
inventory noted earlier, rather than the 3,000–3,500 permitted to be
mated to operational strategic delivery vehicles. Similarly, when the U.S.
Senate ratified START II in 1996, it admonished the president to regulate
the process of reductions so that the number of warheads possessed by
Russia in no case would exceed the number possessed by the United States
to the extent that a strategic imbalance could endanger our security.

It is easy to explain this resistance to changing U.S. nuclear weapons
policies. One important reason is persistent habits left over from the Cold
War—like besting the Soviets in every conceivable category. The rivalry
between the U.S. Air Force and the U.S. Navy to maintain their respective
shares of nuclear forces also came into play at times. There is also the military's tradition of always wanting to have more weapons than one's opponent. Perhaps the ultimate cause, however, is that we have been under
the spell of having tapped the most fundamental source of power, that
which binds atoms together. For the past fifty-three years we have been
fixated on the conclusion that such power can somehow be put to use, despite the fact that neither we nor any other nuclear power has opted to use
this power. Increasingly, though, the view that nuclear weapons are too
powerful to be useful has gained credence. With that, biological and
chemical weapons have begun to be a new locus of concern.

Chemical and biological warfare go back a long ways. In 600 B.C.E. the
Athenians won a battle by poisoning the drinking water of their opposition.
During the Middle Ages, Genghis Khan shot burning pitch and sulfur into
besieged cities, thereby creating asphyxiating clouds of sulfur. During the
fourteenth century, Tartar forces employed cadavers infested with the black
plague as biological agents by vaulting them into the besieged Kaffa (in
present-day Ukraine). During the French and Indian War (1754–1767), the
British created epidemics in several Indian tribes by giving them blankets
that had been used by British soldiers infected with smallpox. And there

have been myriad instances in which the use of chemicals or bacteria was proposed, but nothing came of it. Interestingly, despite the fact that neither of these weapons were employed extensively before World War I, they have long had a reputation for being inhumane, indiscriminate. As far back as 1675 the French and Germans agreed "that no side should use poisoned bullets."[14] In The Hague Conventions of 1899 twenty-four Western nations agreed on a provision against the use of projectiles, "the object of which is diffusion of asphyxiating or deleterious gasses."[15*] A scant sixteen years later, during World War I, these agreed-upon inhibitions went by the board. On April 22, 1915, at the Ypres battlefield, Germany used chlorine, a chemical weapon, for the first time in modern warfare. The attack caused a major rout in the French line, which the Germans failed to exploit due to poor coordination by senior field commanders. The Allied forces responded in kind before the end of the year. The introduction of defensive equipment, such as gas masks, countered the effectiveness of gas by the end of 1916. The Germans, in response, in July of 1917 introduced mustard gas, a blister agent that inflicts casualties by contact with the skin, diminishing the benefits of gas masks. Even this development, though, was not enough to turn the tide of the war. In the end, the effects of chemical warfare, though psychologically demoralizing to troops and civilians, paled in comparison to the destruction of conventional weaponry; of the estimated 20 million casualties in World War I, only about 5 percent (1–1.3 million) were the result of gas warfare.

Nonetheless, there was a general revulsion to this type of warfare, both within the military and the public, which led to postwar efforts to control gas weapons as morally reprehensible. Although several initiatives were attempted, the most enduring agreement reached was the Geneva Protocol of 1925, which was negotiated as part of an international conference attempting to limit trade in arms. The resulting agreement, the "Protocol for the Prohibition of the Use in War of Asphyxiating, Poisonous or Other Gases and of Bacteriological Methods of Warfare," banned the use of chemical and biological weapons, but not their development or production. The Italians broke this ban in Abyssinia during 1935; the Japanese did the same in China

---

*Amusingly, there were two other provisions regarding types of warfare in this Convention. One prohibited the discharge of projectiles from balloons, an effort to keep warfare out of the air. The other prohibited "dum-dum" bullets. The one failed, of course; the other did not.

during 1937. In both cases there was little response from the world community. Still, sufficient taboo remained that during World War II only Japan ventured into chemical and biological warfare, experimenting both on individual Chinese and Chinese cities. These efforts received very little attention.

The fact that there was such limited use of chemical and biological weapons during World War II could have led to the conclusion that the controls established by the Geneva Protocol were adequate. In addition, nuclear weapons had come to overshadow chemical and biological ones. However, interest in controls over chemical and biological weapons did not abate. The Soviet Union helped keep the issue alive by launching a disinformation campaign in 1950 that alleged the United States was employing chemical and biological weapons during the war in Korea. Next, Egypt drew attention to the topic when it used chemical weapons in a civil war in Yemen from 1967–1968. By now we had a United Nations (UN) that picked up and debated the issue. The United States gave impetus to these efforts when President Richard M. Nixon in 1969 renounced first-use of chemical weapons and any use or possession of biological weapons. He did this largely as a matter of conviction, though the fact that the U.S. military had rather little interest in such weapons helped.

Hammering out an international convention on chemical weapons was complicated by continuing accusations of misuse. The United States was again charged with conducting chemical warfare, in the form of defoliants and tear gas during the war in Vietnam. This raised issues of distinctions between weapons, on the one hand, and riot control agents and herbicides on the other. Later the United States accused the Soviet Union and its proxies of employing nerve gas in Afghanistan and so-called yellow rain in Southeast Asia. Hard evidence in cases like these, where the suspected attacks were on a small scale, is difficult to adduce. Currently, most competent observers believe yellow rain was a natural phenomenon. I am troubled, though, by what I saw as Director of Central Intelligence regarding the Soviet role in Afghanistan. There was clear evidence that the Soviets deployed chemical warfare units into Afghanistan in 1980 and established decontamination centers. There could be a simple explanation that such units are part of a package of forces and that nobody thought to hold them back. Yet the Soviets could hardly expect the Afghan guerrillas to be skilled in chemical warfare. Having decontamination facilities immediately available was not very important and had to complicate Soviet logistics.

In 1983 Iraq began employing chemical weapons in its prolonged war with Iran. Initially they were used defensively, against massive waves of infantry attacks, and were not very effective. By 1986, however, the Iraqis had improved their tactics by using chemical weapons in coordination with other weapons to create holes in Iran's defenses. With nonpersistent gas they would cause the Iranians to panic and disperse; then they would advance through the opening. The norm against the use of chemical weapons was weakened in two respects. First, the world community failed in any meaningful way to condemn this breaking of the Geneva Protocol. Even at the end of the war, when Iraq used chemical weapons against rebellious elements within its own citizenry, the Kurds and the Shiites, international condemnation was not forthcoming. Second, Iraq's successful tactical use of poison gas on the battlefield has to make chemical weapons appear attractive to others, whether or not they have signed the CWC.

Chemical weapons, then, are certainly not off the table. Witness that in 1991 the United States was very apprehensive about the possibility of Iraqi use of chemical weapons during the Gulf War. President George Bush had a letter sent to Saddam Hussein, warning, "You and your country will pay a terrible price if you order unconscionable acts of this sort."* The United States prepared its troops for the eventuality of chemical and biological warfare by hastily supplying its forces with defensive equipment and vaccines. After the Gulf War the UN adduced convincing evidence that Iraq, indeed, had possessed the capability for waging extensive chemical warfare during that war. And then in 1995 the Japanese cult Aum Shinrikyo targeted three of Tokyo's subway lines for attack with chemical weapons. They punctured eleven plastic bags containing the chemical nerve agents sarin and cyanide. Twelve people died; 5,500 required medical treatment. It is clear the international community has not yet been able to ensure against future use of chemical agents by engendering a sense of moral disapproval, by creating systems of punishment for their use, and by negotiating enforceable treaties against their use or possession.

There are no examples of the use of biological agents in warfare since the Japanese in World War II. They have been employed as instruments of

---

*Statement by the White House press secretary, Marlin Fitzwater, on President George Bush's letter to President Saddam Hussein of Iraq, January 12, 1991, in *Public Papers of George Bush, Book 1: January 1 to June 20, 1991.*

assassination by intelligence operatives, however. In 1978 Bulgarian agents used an umbrella gun loaded with ricin bullets to kill a Bulgarian defector, Georgi Markov. In 1998 Israeli agents attempted to assassinate Khaled Meshal, a leader of the Islamic militant group Hamas, using a biological agent. Additionally, there are some indications that terrorists have resorted to biological weapons (Aum Shinrikyo reportedly attempted to use aerosol botulinum toxin during the 1995 Tokyo subway attack). Despite this limited record of actual use of biological weapons, two factors have brought them high onto the public's agenda. One is the impressive strides that have been made in biotechnology. Such advancements have opened opportunities of great benefit to humans—but also the possibility of great abuse through the manipulation of cells and genes to create novel and more deadly biological agents. Evidence that the apartheid government of South Africa may have illicitly developed genetically crafted infertility weapons targeting the black population is an ominous indicator of the potential misuse of such advances. The second major factor shaping public attitude on biological warfare in recent years involves the revelations since 1991, as a result of UN weapons inspections, that Iraq had an advanced biological weapons program prior to the Gulf War. The UN inspections have also shown that Iraq is continuing to hide significant elements of its proscribed program. The inspections have revealed not only how much effort and resources Iraq devoted to achieving a biological weapons capability but also how difficult it can be to unearth a concealed program—even with a mandate from the UN Security Council. This and the fact that a number of nations are suspected of having clandestine biological programs—despite being signatories to the BWC—has made biological warfare appear to be closer to reality than theory. One of these is Russia. Back in 1979, well after Russia had signed the BWC, our intelligence detected an outbreak of anthrax in the Soviet city of Sverdlovsk. The Soviets contended this was due to the consumption of poisoned meat. We quickly understood this to be false, as the deaths all occurred in an area directly downwind from a secret research facility.

The appeal of biological weapons comes from the fact that biological agents appear to be many times deadlier, on a pound-for-pound basis, than either chemical or conventional ones, even approaching comparability with nuclear weapons. It is, then, the same spell that nuclear weapons have cast all these years, though here that spell of immense power is founded in theory, not actual demonstration.

Part Two

The Theory

2

POINTS OF
NON-RECOVERY

As Director of Central Intelligence,[1] I was required to brief the Committee on the Armed Services of the House of Representatives annually on the balance of nuclear forces between the United States and the USSR. My first such briefing, in the spring of 1977, consisted of a summation of the numbers and types of nuclear weapons on each side. During the question period, a boyish-looking member from Suffolk County, New York, Tom Downey, complained that my charts, which showed how many of this type of missile the Soviets had and how many of that type we had, were not very edifying. Missiles were not just missiles, he said. One packs more punch than another—for instance, if its guidance system is more accurate. Downey even cited the formula that relates the accuracy and explosive power of a weapon to its total lethality. I didn't know the formula, but I could see his point. I was embarrassed.

I worked with the experts at CIA to devise different ways of comparing the lethal potential of the U.S. and Soviet arsenals. We started from the point that nuclear weapons have two functions: to destroy targets specially hardened against nuclear attack, like the silos in which ICBMs are housed, and to level wide areas of nonhardened structures, like cities or air bases. We compared the theoretical potential of each country in these two operational categories. The Soviets were ahead in each. What was more, they could tip that balance even farther if they attacked first and caught our nuclear forces off their guard. Thus, it was not the prewar balance that would count but how much of our lethal potential would still be available after a surprise, preemptive attack by the Soviets. Would there be enough retaliatory potential to pose a devastating threat? If so, that should deter the Soviets from attempting one. We looked at the worst possible case—assuming they would launch the most disabling attack they could and that we would simply ride it out. We then assessed the number of hard targets and the size of the urban area in the Soviet Union that our surviving nuclear forces would still be able to destroy. The result was revealing and meaningful: No matter what the Soviets did, and despite their being ahead of us quantitatively, the United States could still level the entire urban area of the Soviet Union between one and two times. Put simply, in the worst case imaginable we had much more than enough invulnerable retaliatory force to destroy the Soviet Union as a society. I was encouraged, because I could now tell Downey and his colleagues something relevant to the decisions they had to make.

Alas, the conclusion was all too meaningful for the Pentagon. It sent a clear message that the United States possessed more than enough nuclear weaponry. Yet at that very moment our military was proposing to build still another ICBM, the MX. The rationale was that our existing mix of forces was too vulnerable to surprise attack, something our analysis clearly disputed. The Pentagon's argument against us at CIA, that we in the intelligence field were doing war-gaming and that was not our province, was a sterile bureaucratic ploy.

As we debated this into 1980, I found myself increasingly isolated. Even the CIA's analysts were not behind me. They were concerned not to get the CIA involved in the debate over the MX. There is a strong ethic among intelligence professionals that they must not take sides on policy issues, lest they be accused of slanting the intelligence to support their views. Intelligence analyses, however, must be relevant to policymaking. This one was, and it laid out the facts without taking sides.

In December 1980, despite the objections of the secretary of defense, I sent this analysis to President Carter. It was customary to permit those who dissented with an intelligence report to include their contrary views in it. In this instance, the military intelligence organizations dissented, as did, with my permission, my own staff at CIA. It revealed to me how deeply embedded the view was that more is better. The CIA's analysts, having spent years carefully measuring whether we matched the Soviets in every category of nuclear capability, simply could not countenance being the ones to reveal that we did not need to be equal in order to deter.

Nuclear weapons are not only much more powerful than conventional ones but are also qualitatively different (see Table 2.1). It is not too far-fetched to think of them as small pieces of sun brought to earth, creating effects otherwise not experienced. That nuclear weapons are a species unto themselves is best shown by the terminology we employ to describe their power. The pound is the unit of measure for the explosive in conventional munitions. In contrast, for nuclear munitions the unit of measure is the metric tonne (2,200 pounds), but the weapons are so powerful that we refer to their force in kilotons (KT—thousands of tonnes) and even megatons (MT—millions of tonnes). Five hundred pounds of TNT is the explosive force of a common conventional bomb; in contrast, a typical warhead in Russia's strategic arsenal carries 550 KT of force. A 550-KT weapon is the equivalent of 550 × 1,000 (kilo) × 2,200 (lbs./metric tonne), that is, 1,210,000,000 pounds of conventional explosive. A freight train 150 miles long would be needed to transport that much conventional explosive to an airfield. It would take more than 25,000 sorties by our most modern bomber, the B-2, to deliver it. In the course of some 44,000 aircraft sorties during the six-week air campaign in the Gulf War in 1991, we dropped only 84,000 metric tonnes of conventional bombs, or less than one-fifth of the explosive force of a single 550-KT nuclear bomb.[2]

It is understandable that we prefer to use MT and KT instead of ten-figure numerals when referring to the force of nuclear weapons; the acronyms are much handier. Doing so, however, has encouraged us to talk rather cavalierly about the magnitude of the power involved. For instance, it is not so incongruous to talk about a "small" nuclear warhead when we label it as .1 KT. A warhead of that lethality is small enough to fit in an artillery shell but is the equivalent of .1 × 1,000 (kilo) × 2,200 (lbs./tonne), or 220,000 pounds of conventional explosive. That means that every time a nuclear artillery shell is fired it is the same as launching five fully loaded B-2 bombers at the target.

We must, however, be careful. Equating 550 KT of nuclear explosive with 1.2 billion pounds of conventional explosive, or .1 KT of nuclear

TABLE 2.1   Comparative Effects of Nuclear and Conventional Weapons, (range in miles)

	Conventional 500-lb. Bomb	.1 KT (artillery shell)	12.5 KT (Hiroshima)	250 KT (U.S. ICBM)	550 KT (Russian ICBM)
Blast[a]					
Knock down unreinforced brick buildings	0.02	0.43	1	2.7	3.5
Thermal[b]					
Ignite wooden buildings	None[c]	.24–.34	.8–1.2	4–5	6–7
Radioactivity[d]					
Lethal to 50 percent of people exposed	None	5–10	15–30	50–100	75–150

[a]Nuclear blast ranges are computed assuming that the weapon height of burst has been adjusted to give 5 psi overpressure over the largest possible area.

[b]The ranges quoted here are for ten and twenty calories per square centimeter on the ground. At these ranges, fires will be initiated by the light-flash from the nuclear fireball.

[c]The blast wave from a 500-pound bomb could cause fires by knocking over stoves or by causing electrical shorts or broken gas lines. However, unlike a nuclear explosion, the bomb does not create a light-flash intense enough to set fires directly.

[d]In order for there to be significant fallout from a nuclear detonation, the explosion must occur on the ground or near the surface. The blast effects in the first row assume heights of burst that would not, in most circumstances, result in substantial early fallout. Depending on wind conditions, the actual distances where fallout from near-surface bursts could pose a serious threat of injury or to life could be larger or smaller. The downwind distances cited here should only be used as a means of establishing a rough scale of distance for serious fallout.

with 220,000 pounds of conventional, greatly understates the difference, because such comparisons account for only the blast effects of the two kinds of weapons and ignore four additional effects of nuclear weapons:

- An extraordinarily intense flash of light and heat can kill people and ignite fires miles from the point of detonation. These fires, which occur within milliseconds, can initiate firestorms over areas of tens to hundreds of square miles with average air temperatures well above the boiling point of water and average wind speeds of hurricane force. The high winds can overturn flammables like stoves and gasoline pumps and start additional fires. Overturned stoves are believed to have been the major source of fires at Hiroshima.[3]
- There will be enormous amounts of radioactivity. Immediate, direct radiation from a 550-KT airburst, that is, where the fireball

explodes above and does not touch the ground, can kill people within several miles. When the fireball does touch the ground, radioactivity attached to particles lifted into the air by the explosion could carry, depending on wind conditions and other factors, literally around the globe and be deposited tens, hundreds, even thousands of miles from the explosion. Because the effects of radioactivity vary widely with weather, wind, and the nature of the soil and infrastructure at ground zero, they can only be approximated. Typically, it has been estimated that a 1-MT detonation near the ground at the center of Detroit would contaminate a cigar-shaped zone reaching as far as Pittsburgh, 250 miles away. Some areas within that zone would be too contaminated to inhabit for periods ranging from a few days to ten years; for example, an area about 200 miles by 100 miles would be uninhabitable for one month, an area about 100 miles by ten miles for a year. (The modest explosion at the Chernobyl nuclear power plant in the Soviet Union in 1986 deposited radioactive material some 1,500 miles away in Norway; reindeer there became so contaminated from eating the vegetation that they were not fit for human consumption.) Additionally, an area around a groundburst cannot be inhabited for years (e.g., an area of 1,200 square miles adjacent to the Chernobyl plant has been uninhabitable since the explosion, and some 30,000 square miles of farmland can be only partially cultivated).[4] Because radioactivity can carry so far, any groundburst will endanger cities, even if detonation occurs on a remote military target. Russian ICBM silos are so hardened, for instance, that U.S. plans for destroying them at times called for employing two large, near-groundburst warheads. That would send a massive amount of radioactive particles into the atmosphere. In the Soviet Union, some ICBM silos were directly upwind of major cities, including Moscow. There are fewer Russian ICBMs so located today, but any major attack on them would still cause serious contamination problems in cities.

• An electromagnetic pulse (EMP) of thousands of volts can be expected to overload electrical circuits and disrupt or destroy power, communications, and computer networks and other critical electrical systems. A single, deliberate EMP burst high over

the center of the United States would likely cause a temporary
electrical and communications blackout nationwide.

• Environmental damage of several sorts is likely. Since trees and
many other plants are roughly as susceptible to radiation exposure
as are people, any area exposed to levels of radiation high enough
to kill or injure people would be deforested or depleted of plant
life. This, in turn, would have implications for soil erosion and for
the survival prospects of wildlife and domesticated animals. For
example, insects, which are more resistant to radiation than birds,
would no longer be as subject to predators. This, in turn, could
lead to wild fluctuations in the size of insect populations in the
new ecological system created by the elimination of predators and
plant life. Numerous nuclear explosions could also create
sufficient nitric oxides to deplete the ozone layer twenty to thirty
kilometers above the earth. This would expose humans and
animals to higher than normal ultraviolet radiation. Although the
physics of ozone depletion is not fully understood, the
consequences of it could be serious. There is also the thesis of
"nuclear winter," which holds that vast fires started by a large
nuclear attack would cause smoke and particles in the atmosphere
to cut off the sun's rays for an extended period, with a subsequent
cooling effect. Although the surface temperature change might not
be as severe as suggested in early analyses of the potential for
nuclear winter, there are enough effects associated with nuclear
winter that it cannot be discounted entirely.

All of these unique effects of nuclear weapons have been and still are either totally ignored or severely discounted in U.S. government estimates
of nuclear damage. It is true that these effects all vary with conditions
such as weather, time of day, terrain, the way the weapons are detonated,
and the amount of shelter for humans. But just because effects can vary
does not mean we can ignore them. Yet the U.S. government has just
about done that by relying almost exclusively on the effects of blast,
thereby seriously underestimating the total lethality of nuclear weapons.
There are, for instance, conflagration models estimating that deaths
caused by fires would be 1.5–4.1 times greater than the government calcu-
lates. Overall, in my opinion, the U.S. government underestimates nuclear
damage by a factor of at least two and in some instances by one of eight,

depending on the particular circumstance.* This amount of uncertainty as to the effects of nuclear detonations, plus the enormity of even the smallest of them, make it virtually impossible to develop plans for employing them with any precision.

Common sense tells us that it would have been difficult to employ the 32,500 warheads we once had in our arsenal, 13,000 of them being of intercontinental range and each roughly thirty times as powerful as the bomb used at Hiroshima. The entire Soviet bloc had less than 250 cities with populations greater than 100,000, which would have meant fifty-two warheads per city. Needless to say, multiple nuclear detonations on the 250 largest population centers would damage that society beyond recognition, just as Carthage was obliterated in 146 B.C. by Scipio Africanus, a Roman who not only conquered Carthage's army and razed the city but also placed a curse on its fields and sowed them with salt. The release of 13,000 nuclear warheads would, in effect, also sow salt in our own fields and those of many other nations because of contaminating radioactive fallout. The overkill this number of warheads represented was evident quite early. President Dwight Eisenhower commented back in 1959, when we had many fewer weapons, that military leaders were "trying to get themselves into an incredible position of having enough to destroy every conceivable target all over the world, plus a three-fold reserve."[5]

Because this was so obvious without any elaborate studies or calculations, the United States and Soviet Union decided during the early 1960s to commence negotiating arms control agreements. Those agreements have brought us to the current objective of each having 3,000–3,500 warheads mated to delivery vehicles by 2007. One way to think about what 3,000 nuclear warheads could do to our nation is to hypothesize an all-out Russian attack distributed evenly among the fifty states (a conceptual strategy for illustrative purposes only). That means sixty warheads per state. Even if the warheads were distributed randomly, the impact would be unimaginable in Rhode Island and still a catastrophe in Alaska. And if the warheads were deliberately aimed at the sixty largest cities in each state, our country certainly would be another Carthage. Similarly, Russia today has roughly 200 cities with populations over 100,000; 3,000 U.S. warheads, or sixteen per city, would carry it far past survival.

---

*A more detailed explanation of this contention is in Appendix A.

This is a worst-case scenario because it deliberately targets the most valuable assets: people and their places of work or living. There is an argument that attacking cities would be immoral. There is a counterargument that deliberately threatening cities and people would not be immoral because it would make it so abundantly clear how disastrous nuclear war would be that deterrence would be reinforced. As noted earlier, the world of nations has, however, been moving for almost a century toward outlawing the more horrific forms of warfare, such as poison gas, biological agents, dum-dum bullets, and the indiscriminate killing of civilians. Nuclear attacks on cities would unquestionably fall into the category of horrific; therefore, developing plans to attack them deliberately could be more than our consciences would allow.

One alternative the United States has adopted, supposedly on moral grounds, is to target only military or military-industrial facilities, not cities. Curiously, this happens to accord with a doctrine enunciated more than 150 years ago by the famed military strategist Carl von Clausewitz: The main target for an army is usually the enemy's army; that is, defeating the enemy's military forces is normally the best route to victory.[6] The idea of threatening only military targets also fits neatly with the thinking of many civilians involved in developing nuclear strategy. Their quest has been to find if there are ways to make using nuclear weapons acceptable. Any that destroyed too much would not be acceptable. For instance, President Eisenhower was so shocked because it was estimated that 285 million Russians and Chinese would die if our entire nuclear force was launched at them.[7] So to avoid such concerns with morality, we came to build our war plans around targeting largely military installations or military-related industries. Much of the early developmental work on such targeting strategies was done by a civilian group at RAND. Civilians like these play a much larger role in nuclear strategy than in conventional strategy because they need not defer to the experience and judgment of military officers. A former RAND analyst once stated it succinctly: "General, I have fought just as many nuclear wars as you have."[8]

But there is a problem with the military-target strategy: It demands many more weapons to pose a sufficient threat to deter. Essentially, it is the difference between aiming many weapons at military targets of modest value or a few weapons at civilian targets (i.e., cities) of great value. Besides, there are large numbers of military targets in countries like Russia and China, and being ready to destroy only a modest percentage of them

would not necessarily intimidate sufficiently to deter. The most fundamental problem, however, is that many nuclear weapons aimed at military
targets will inevitably damage cities and their residents also.

There is a middle ground between the hypocrisy of pretending to target
only military targets and the perceived immorality of targeting cities. Useful work on this was done at Massachusetts Institute of Technology (MIT)
in 1987 by a group under Dr. Kosta Tsipis, who employed a computer
model of the U.S. economy to evaluate the effects of various sizes and
kinds of nuclear attacks on the United States. * This group introduced hypothetical disruptions in economic activity as a result of attacks from nuclear weapons. The model was dynamic and reflected the secondary effects of the loss of the various activities destroyed. The study found that
the United States is particularly vulnerable to attacks on the sources of
and the distribution network for liquid fuel: refineries, oil fields, control
centers for pipelines for gas and oil, and harbors. Some of these targets,
like harbors, are clearly within cities; some, like refineries, oil fields, and
key points in the pipeline systems, can be away from population centers.

The simulation showed that as a result of 239 nuclear detonations aimed
at our liquid fuel system, gross national product (GNP) returned to only 40
percent of the preattack level after six years; and 60 percent of the population had died within two years. Both projections were largely the result of a
breakdown of the nation's transportation network because of shortages of
gasoline, diesel oil, and aviation fuel. Food supplies did not get through and
people starved; components manufactured in one city for factories in other
cities did not reach them; imported raw materials were prevented from
reaching their destinations, which in turn slowed deliveries of other products; and so on down the chain. It is particularly noteworthy that the MIT
study made numerous optimistic assumptions, for example, that the national communications system would remain sufficiently intact for the government to direct the recovery effort and that national morale would hold
up enough so that people would respond to directions.

The MIT approach meets the test of common sense. Just imagine the impacts if fuel was no longer readily available in U.S. cities. With electricity
limited, workplace productivity would drop; with reduced availability of
water, medical services, and sewage treatment, health would be endangered;

---

*An excerpt from this study describing the methodology and results is included in
Appendix B.

and with limits on gasoline, public and private transportation would have to be curtailed with effects ranging from reduced supplies for factories, to workers not being able to commute, to garbage not being collected.

The U.S. government's role in the MIT study is very telling. The dynamic model was developed by a private company on contract to the Federal Emergency Management Agency (FEMA), the organization responsible for civil recovery from nuclear attacks. As it became clear that the results from employing this model would undercut statements like that of Secretary of Defense Caspar Weinberger—that we could win a nuclear war—FEMA withdrew its support. The MIT group took over the model from the contractor and worked on it. When that group released its conclusions about the hypothetical attack of 239 weapons, FEMA repudiated it with a bland statement that the computer model was too sensitive to some economic variables, such as interest rates.[9]

The lesson from the MIT study is that the lasting impact of multiple nuclear detonations upon an economy and a society would be far greater than the sum of individual blasts. The ability of any urban area to recover from a nuclear attack would depend on outside assistance, as at Hiroshima and Nagasaki. But if those sources of assistance had been attacked and required assistance themselves, the recovery would be prolonged. Estimating such secondary effects is very difficult, but they are real. The 239 detonations in the MIT study would protract the time it would take to restore our economy, government structure, and social institutions to the point that when the society did revive it would not be recognizable. Many democratic and humanitarian values would be set aside while we struggled with primary needs. If the nation's transportation net was crippled, the national economy might divide into regional economies. Our tightly integrated industrial economy might give way to a more agrarian one. Given regional agrarian economies, new internal political alignments would likely develop. And with medical resources severely overstrained, human relations could become dangerously confrontational. For instance, one sizable nuclear detonation over a major city could create more burn casualties than all the specialized burn facilities in the entire country could handle.[10] The greater the number of deaths, both instant and lingering, the more likely the psychological trauma would lead to despair and loss of will to recover. The prolonged struggle for basic survival and recovery could eclipse any substantive U.S. role in world affairs.

Society would have passed what we might term its *point of non-recovery*. Determining what amount of damage would constitute the point of non-recovery for the United States is, of course, a subjective matter. The 239 detonations on liquid fuel supplies, as in the MIT study, would seem to be sufficient. We need to pursue and refine such studies, not just reject them out of hand, as did FEMA, if we are to make sensible decisions on nuclear policy.

Russia is also vulnerable to being pushed past a point of non-recovery. Russia is larger in area than the United States and, therefore, more dependent on transportation links, but those links rely on coal more than on liquid fuel. Russia's industry is not as highly developed as that of the United States, but it is concentrated in fewer locations. Whether threatening its transportation and communications systems would be the best approach to deterring Russia could also only be determined by doing specific, dynamic computer simulations. Still, there is no reason to suggest that some threat of about 250 warheads on some vital national systems would not put Russia into the category of being beyond the point of non-recovery.

China must also have a point of non-recovery, but estimating it is more difficult. With its immense population and largely agrarian economy, China is less vulnerable than Russia and the United States to starvation and industrial interruption from a breakdown in transportation. China does have more limited transportation, electric power, and communications systems. Breakdowns in them could foster the breakup of the country into regional groupings as central authority became weakened. Again, specific simulations would need to be run, but China's vulnerability appears to be more political than economic. One possible indicator of China's thinking in regard to national vulnerabilities is that China has thus far limited the size of its nuclear forces that can reach the United States to less than thirty warheads and to central and western Russia to less than a few hundred. This could be the result of deliberate decisions to allocate limited high-technology resources elsewhere. There are, though, indicators the Chinese are more interested in qualitative improvements to their nuclear arsenal than to quantitative increases—that is, they apparently believe enough damage can be done to countries like Russia and the United States with only modest nuclear forces to deter them from initiating nuclear war. Short of thorough study, it is not unreasonable to believe that about 250 nuclear detonations would also place China beyond the point of non-recovery.

Smaller nations are vulnerable to far fewer nuclear detonations because of the limited number of transportation, communication, and industrial systems. Their societies and economies could be drastically disrupted with relatively few nuclear detonations on key industrial plants, natural resources, and government facilities. Perhaps the most limiting factor would be a moral question: Would there be enough targets outside of cities, or would any attempt to push them beyond the point of non-recovery be tantamount to attacking the entire society, including its population?

An MIT-type strategy of threatening vital national systems would not solve the moral problems of nuclear deterrence but would be morally preferable to a strategy of deliberate attacks on cities. It would also move us away from our fixation with the Clausewitzian dictum that defeating an enemy's military forces is the key to winning wars. That rationale has inflated our requirements for nuclear forces beyond reason and has led us into planning to wage nuclear wars in the image of conventional ones. It has also forced us to assume that if we are targeting Russia's nuclear forces they must be targeting ours and, hence, we must take the risks of being on hair-trigger alert lest they catch us by surprise. There is no element in U.S. nuclear policy more corrosive to rational policymaking than our adherence to the dictum that the objective in nuclear war must be to destroy the opponent's nuclear forces.

In addition, embracing an MIT-type strategy would remind us there is no need to threaten any nation all the way to extinction in order to deter. Threatening to push a nation past its point of non-recovery through attacks on various vital systems, such as liquid fuel supplies, should be more than adequate to deter or to do whatever amount of damage we might conceivably find it necessary to do. We need to study just what it would take to do that to various potential opponents. Whether it is specifically 250 or 500 or even 1,000 detonations is not important today, because all of those limits are far below our current target in START II of 3,500 warheads, let alone the 10,000 we intend actually to retain.

Alas, any suggestion that the United States needs only a few hundred nuclear warheads typically meets with vehement opposition. One standard objection is that we need to be prepared for more than one nuclear war. One example of this would be if we and the Russians each exhausted all of a limited number of nuclear warheads in a war with each other and the Chinese then stepped in and attacked either or both of us with nuclear forces. This is a case of extrapolating a possibility of conventional warfare to nuclear warfare without considering the order of magnitude of difference in the amounts of destruction. In this hypothetical situation, the United States and Russia, having pushed one another past their points of non-recovery, would require decades to rebuild economies, societies, and military power before being able again to threaten China or anyone else. Why would China want to engage either with nuclear weapons? It would already have been vaulted toward being the preeminent world power. For the sake of damaging us even more seriously, China would be taking an enormous risk, as we might have just one surviving submarine with its load of missiles. China would be deterred because the potential gains would not be worth the risks.

Another objection to keeping only a minimum inventory of warheads is that we may need reserves in case a group of warheads deteriorates in peacetime or fails to perform in war. This argument is applicable only when the strategy requires hitting precise numbers of targets. When the strategy is to push an opponent past a point of non-recovery, a few detonations more or less are not significant. If we truly believed our retaliatory forces had deteriorated (and they never have in a significant way during the past fifty-plus years) we would shift our targeting toward higher-value targets to ensure being able to threaten non-recovery. At the same time, we should keep in mind that the point of non-recovery is not precise. It is not like military targeting, where the difference between destroying 100 percent of an opponent's ICBMs, for instance, and only 90 percent could be vital. The MIT study concluded there would be a loss of 60 percent of the population after two years, but it would hardly make much difference if it turned out to be only 50 percent.

But the most fundamental reason some people oppose a minimum inventory is a deep-seated concern with falling behind the Russians in any category of nuclear capability. The most strident voices are those expressing fear that our retaliatory forces could be overwhelmed: What if we went to 250 warheads and the Russians abrogated START II and retained, say, 7,000? Any reasonable person would be concerned with a 25:1 adverse ratio of nuclear forces, even if our retaliatory force was totally safe from attack. A 25:1 ratio, however, is a bogus case. After all these years of focusing on parity in our negotiations on arms control and in our decisions on force levels, it would be politically impossible, let alone just plain imprudent, for us to allow such a wide differential to develop. At any reasonable ratio we would have no cause to worry that the Russians could locate and destroy all of our nuclear forces before enough of them could launch a retaliatory attack that would carry Russia to its point of non-recovery. (Just why this is so is discussed in Chapter 7.)

Concern with being overwhelmed, then, is more a stalking horse for a deep-seated conviction that superiority in these weapons affords us prestige on the world stage and political leverage over the Russians. Many nuclear strategists point to the Berlin crises of 1958 and 1963 as evidence that our nuclear superiority forced Nikita Khrushchev to back down. Yet they slight the fact that during the 1961 Cuban missile crisis President John Kennedy made concessions to the Soviets in spite of the fact that he knew he was playing from a vastly superior nuclear hand.

In understanding whether there was nuclear leverage in cases like these, we need to differentiate between nuclear superiority and nuclear danger.[11] If Khrushchev was influenced by the nuclear imbalance, it was not because he feared his country would come out second-best in a nuclear exchange: It was because he knew his country would be devastated in the absolute, regardless of the relative amount of damage to the United States. Similarly, if Kennedy was unwilling to press his nuclear superiority, it was because his focus was on the absolute damage the United States might receive, not the much greater damage we could certainly do to the Soviet Union. In short, both leaders were deterred by the absolute danger their countries faced. Perceptions of nuclear superiority or inferiority did not afford leverage in those political showdowns. The importance of recognizing there is a point of non-recovery with nuclear weapons is that it helps define a limit on the number any nation could require.

With biological and chemical weapons, the question is whether either type of weapon could do enough damage to a country like the United States to push it to the point of non-recovery. There is little empirical data on which to base such a judgment. In addition, with both biological and chemical weapons there is greater uncertainty in estimates of lethality than with nuclear weapons. There are more factors that can substantially effect lethality, for example, whether the weather is clear or cloudy, whether it is daytime or night, whether the agents in the weapons are stable enough to survive delivery in the precise form needed to injure, and whether there are defensive preparations (see Table 2.2).

TABLE 2.2   Estimated Lethality of a Single Chemical Weapon Delivered on an Urban Area

	Least Favorable Case	*Moderately Favorable Case*	*Highly Favorable Case*
Agent and amount	30 kg. of sarin nerve gas	1000 kg. of sarin nerve gas	1000 kg. of sarin nerve gas
Delivery means	Missile	Aircraft aerosol spraying	Aircraft aerosol spraying
Weather	Overcast, moderate wind	Overcast, moderate wind	Night—no wind
Expected fatalities	60–200	400–800	3,000–8,000

Chemical agents are poisons that kill or injure through immediate toxic effects on lungs, blood, eyes, nerves, and other organs. An individual must come into direct contact with a sufficient amount of an agent to be killed. If, as shown in Table 2.2, a high number of deaths to be expected from one chemical weapon is 8,000, it would take an inordinate number of chemical weapons to carry the United States beyond recovery (certainly in comparison with the 239 nuclear detonations estimated by the study at MIT). That conclusion, however, is dependent on the validity of the data in Table 2.2. The Office of Technology Assessment (OTA) of the U.S. Congress calculated them in 1993. OTA has no perceptible reason to be either alarmist or complacent. There are, though, more alarmist calculations. To allow for this, another test would be to increase the OTA's highest estimate by a factor of, say, ten. That would result in a maximum of 80,000 fatalities per chemical weapon if delivered by aerosol spraying at night with no wind. At that point the controlling factors would be the ability of any aggressor to deliver what would still be a very large number of these weapons while consistently achieving the maximum lethality per weapon. In my view, that is out of the question. Thus, chemical weapons, although as odious as their reputation, are not truly weapons of mass destruction, that is, they do not have the potential to destroy a major nation, something we believed, during the Cold War, the Soviet Union had as regards the United States if it used nuclear weapons. Chemical agents, then, are not likely to be a weapon of choice by a major power for an all-out attack on the United States or any other major power.

Biological agents are many times deadlier than chemical agents on a pound-for-pound basis (see Table 2.3). They are disease-causing microorganisms that multiply within the infected person. Thus, over time they become more lethal unless countered with an antidote. Of even more concern, some biological agents, such as smallpox, are contagious and can spread widely and indiscriminately.

The highest estimate of 3 million potential fatalities from a biological weapon make such weapons appear to be competitive with nuclear weapons (e.g., the OTA's high-end estimate for a 500-KT nuclear weapon is 1.9 million). Biological weapons, though, are not truly competitive with nuclear weapons, because the uncertainties of achieving the predicted lethality are so much greater. And biological weapons depend solely on killing people or crops, whereas the physical destruction of infrastructure by nuclear weapons can generate much more economic and societal disruption. Beyond that, we cannot legitimately scale up the lethality of individual chemical or biological weapons to a nationwide attack. The only practical way to deliver them on a scale that would threaten entire cities is via aerosol spraying. It would be immensely difficult for an aggressor, even with biological weapons, to send sufficient aircraft, trucks, or any other delivery vehicles to enough U.S. cities to immobilize the country without being detected and stopped.

The risks of not achieving a very high level of destruction are too great for biological weapons to be a major power's choice for attacking another major power. Nuclear weapons would be the preferred option. Nonnuclear powers, however, could conceivably decide biological weapons were the best way to attack a major power. They would, though, be accepting enormous risks, because they could not conduct an attack on such a scale covertly. The possibility of having to suffer nuclear or other substantial retaliation would loom large. Biological weapons, then, have the potential to be weapons of mass destruction in the sense of pushing major nations past their points of non-recovery only theoretically. As a practical matter, they are not a rational option. The most likely exception to this would be the use of a biological agent that was virulently contagious, for example, smallpox. A smaller number of such weapons might do enormous damage over time. Such an act would not only be irresponsible; it would also be dangerous. The disease could easily spread to other countries than the one attacked, even affecting the attacker's own territory. Irrationality and

TABLE 2.3   Estimated Lethality of a Single Biological Weapon Delivered on an Urban Area

	Least Favorable Case	*Moderately Favorable Case*	*Highly Favorable Case*
Agent and amount	30 kg. of anthrax spores	100 kg. of anthrax spores	100 kg. of anthrax spores
Delivery means	Missile	Aircraft aerosol spraying	Aircraft aerosol spraying
Weather	Overcast, moderate wind	Overcast, moderate wind	Night—no wind
Expected fatalities	30,000– 100,000	420,000– 1,400,000	1,000,000– 3,000,000

irresponsibility cannot be ruled out, but at least the probability of contagious biological attacks is narrowed to fanatics.

Scoping the upper side of the potential for biological warfare is important because there is considerable controversy today over how great a danger biological and chemical weapons present. That there is uncertainty over the lethality of biological weapons should not be a surprise. The OTA data estimates in Table 2.3 show the lethal effects of biological weapons under least favorable conditions to be smaller by a factor of 100 than under optimal conditions. Thus, individuals who focus on the upper end can be almost in panic over this threat. Others who concentrate on the low end are convinced it is a threat being blown out of proportion.

As a result, there is a danger of either overestimating or underestimating, but more likely overestimating. For instance, in early 1998 Secretary of Defense William Cohen appeared on TV and talked about the dangers of biological warfare. He placed a five-pound bag of sugar on the table in front of him and announced that were it filled with anthrax spores, they could kill one-half the population of Washington, D.C. That graphic illustration grabbed the attention of viewers, indeed. It may have served a purpose in drawing public attention to the issue of biological warfare. There are, though, fundamental problems with Cohen's approach.

His statement is incomplete and, therefore, misleading. Had he placed any ordinary weapon on the table, the majority of us would have assumed that it had a given lethality: a bullet normally kills one individual; a 500-pound bomb has some lethal radius; a 500-KT nuclear bomb still a different one.

We all recognize that someone has to aim the weapon correctly or the bullet will not kill anyone, and even the 500-KT nuclear blast will not do the destruction expected if it detonates too far from its aim point. What did not come through with the bag of sugar analogy is that there can be a huge variation in the lethality of five pounds of anthrax spores due to a number of variables, over and above accuracy of delivery:

- The spores must be prepared for an aerosol spray to achieve maximum effectiveness. That means freeze-drying them and then precisely milling the granules to a size of one to five microns (a micron is one-millionth of a meter, less than the width of a hair). Larger sizes generally do not stay airborne long enough to spread widely and be inhaled.
- The milled spores must be stabilized lest they lose their lethality in storage, transportation, and delivery.
- Delivery requires a finely calibrated spraying machine to release enough, but not many, of the minute particles so as to maximize the area covered with a lethal dose.
- Spraying of any sizable area almost has to be done by a low-flying aircraft. Because this is so abnormal over major cities, it is likely to attract attention. That, in turn, could lead to taking defensive measures and stopping additional spraying.
- Weather conditions during the spraying substantially impact the survival and distribution of the spores. Sunlight will kill some; wind will scatter them and dilute the dosage.
- Lethality will be affected by how vulnerable the population happens to be to anthrax. Some individuals could have had anthrax vaccinations; some could be treated afterwards and survive; and some may be naturally less susceptible to anthrax.

Additionally, Cohen's numbers differ substantially from the more generally accepted calculations of the Office of Technology Assessment from which Table 2.3 is derived. The largest estimate of fatalities in Table 2.3 is 3 million. That, though, was premised on the use of 200 pounds of anthrax spores, not five. Scaled to five pounds, the OTA fatalities would be only 68,000 compared with Cohen's 300,000. The smallest OTA forecast when scaled to five pounds of anthrax spores is only 2,200. Yet if you hypothesize somehow being able to distribute five pounds of anthrax across the population of the United States in a clinical fashion so that each person received only the precise, minimal amounts for lethality, we would all die.

In short, there is an extremely wide divergence between perfectly honest estimates of the lethality of biological weapons. In largest measure this is due to differing assumptions as to how the biological agents are administered and under what conditions. It is also due to the fact that there is very little empirical data about the lethality of anthrax with humans. We experiment on monkeys, not people. One shaky data point on humans is the Soviet accident at Sverdlovsk in 1979. Unfortunately, we do not know how much anthrax was released or its form. We are not even certain of the number of deaths. The best estimate, though, is that less than 100 people were killed in a plume that went downwind over an urban area and well into the countryside to where the last sheep was known to have died of anthrax. Unless the release was absolutely minute, lethality was less than is often suggested. That kind of data prompt some individuals to believe the threat of biological warfare is being exaggerated.

What all this tells us is that we must judge carefully where to target our efforts against biological threats. If we accept the extremely pessimistic estimates, it will appear futile to do anything. If we accept the opposite, minimal extreme, we will also do nothing. We must aim somewhere in the middle and continually adjust the amount and type of effort we make, as we better understand the danger.

3

POINTS OF
SELF-DETERRENCE

IN EARLY 1979, Major General Jasper A. Welch of the U.S. Air Force
came to the CIA to brief me and several agency experts on nuclear arms
control. The subject was the basing plan for the proposed MX ICBM. Ostensibly, the issue was how to locate the MX to make it less vulnerable
than the current missiles, which were housed in highly visible concrete silos throughout remote areas of the United States. The general described
the "racetrack" plan that had been selected by the Department of Defense
after exploring some twenty alternatives, which included carrying the
missiles in aircraft, placing them on railroads, hiding them in tunnels, and
anchoring them on the bottom of the sea. In this plan we would build
forty-three fixed shelters around oval, concrete tracks, each about twenty
miles long and ten miles wide. There would be 200 separate tracks, all located in the deserts of Nevada. The individual shelters would be hardened
with enough concrete that a 1-MT nuclear weapon could destroy only the
shelter it targeted. In just one of the shelters on each track there would be
a single MX mounted on a wheeled transporter vehicle.

The concept was to move the missile from one shelter to another between the time we detected an incoming missile attack and its arrival.
This was all to be done automatically; that is, there would be no humans
on the transporter. At the flip of a switch in a control center the transporter and its missile, weighing in at some 500,000 pounds combined,
would move out and dash around the track. A guidance system embedded

in the track would lead it to any of the other forty-two shelters. I was dumbfounded by this far-fetched scheme.

I was reviewing it because President Carter wanted to know whether making the MX safe from surprise attack in this manner might also make it impossible for the Soviets to check on the total number of MXs we had. The Soviet Union would be entitled under SALT II, the strategic arms limitation treaty that was then under negotiation, to use photographic satellites to verify the number of U.S. ICBMs. How would they be able to determine the number of missiles that were hidden in each set of forty-three shelters? Somehow we had to make our MXs both invisible and visible. General Welch told us the plan was to install large doors on top of the shelters and open all 43 of them periodically during times Soviet photographic satellites passed overhead. After studying this, the CIA experts concluded the Soviets did have the ability to peer into these openings and ascertain whether a missile was housed there or not.

I had to bite my tongue in concurring with that evaluation because it would help this wild scheme move forward, but I could not resist chiding the general just a bit. Early in the briefing he had noted that to placate opposition from environmentalists, the Air Force would open the tracks to public use. He said they would be ideal for drag racing. I asked, "What if there were people out there drag racing when that half-million-pound vehicle with nobody on board is suddenly launched out onto the track?" Unperturbed, he responded that any humans on the track might well be run over. He contended that it wouldn't matter because we would only launch that vehicle if we were convinced a Soviet nuclear missile was headed to that very track. Anyone on it was going to die anyway. I was nonplused at this prepared, coldly calculated response and at a loss as to what to say.

THERE IS A COMPULSION TO USE NUCLEAR WEAPONS, but because of their very power there is also a constraint. How could we ever have been serious about a scheme like the MX racetrack? Yet when the Reagan administration took over the MX program two years later, the racetrack plan was replaced by one even more absurd. In "Dense Pack," 100 MX missiles would be clustered tightly together. An attack on any one would throw up so much debris as to destroy the follow-on attacking missiles aimed at the other ninety-nine. Presumably those ninety-nine would survive long enough to be launched after the debris had settled. This approach to being safe by inviting attack garnered the title "Dunce Pack." Congress laughed it out of being. Incredibly, we ended up placing MXs in existing silos, where they remain every bit as vulnerable as those they replaced.

This obsession with the MX, then, was not a quest for lesser vulnerability but one for a more powerful ICBM. That conveyed the impression that what we wanted was to enhance our capability for waging nuclear war. Back then ICBMs were the best war-fighting nuclear weapons, as they were unmatched in terms of carrying capacity, accuracy, and responsiveness to an order to shoot.* Our ICBM force, though, was inferior to that of the Soviets in total amount of destructive potential. Despite the fact that nuclear missiles do not engage enemy nuclear missiles as, for instance, tanks fight enemy tanks, that discrepancy galled our nuclear strategists.

Having the best war-fighting capability is seen as important because of the dictum of Clausewitz that "war is not a mere act of policy, but a true political instrument, a continuation of political activity by other means."[1] If war is to be employed to further policy, political leaders must feel confident they will win. Historically, they have asked whether their military was capable of doing more damage to the opponent than the opponent to them, with particular emphasis on doing more harm to enemy military forces. When analyzing inside the nuclear sphere, however, political leaders ask a different question, as Khrushchev and Kennedy did during the Berlin and Cuban crises: whether the damage their country would receive in retaliation could possibly be acceptable. Pushing an opponent past its point of non-recovery two or three times would be without satisfaction if you are pushed there even once as a result. It is only common sense, then, that at some point prospective damage to oneself will inhibit the will to initiate the use of nuclear weapons. That point is identified as the *point of self-deterrence.*

The *point of non-recovery* defines the maximum number of nuclear weapons that a nation could usefully employ against another nation without going to excess. The *point of self-deterrence* defines the level of nuclear damage in retaliation that would deter a nation from initiating nuclear war.

Points of self-deterrence will vary with a country's international position, objectives, culture, and form of government. During the Cold War we im-

---

*Technological developments have since made the sea-launched ballistic missile comparable in these categories of performance.

plicitly accepted the idea that it might be necessary to absorb considerable nuclear damage to the United States as a result of employing nuclear weapons in defense of European allies. As risky as this was, we believed this bluff was the most rational option we had. In the post–Cold War world, in contrast, our point of self-deterrence is as low as one nuclear detonation on our soil or against U.S. military forces overseas. There is no objective of foreign policy today that is so threatened that we would employ nuclear weapons to defend it at the risk of receiving just one nuclear detonation in retaliation. We have only to look at the situations where the United States has made substantial military commitments since World War II:

- Western Europe: There is no longer a conventional military threat to our West European allies that they and we could not handle together.
- The Korean Peninsula: North Korea, with only one-eighth of the gross domestic product (GDP) of South Korea and one-half its population, although still a dangerous opponent, could not hope to win in any sustained combat.
- Vietnam: This country has long been off our list of vital concerns.
- The Mideast: A lesson of the Gulf War in 1991 is that we can protect our access to oil in the Mideast without deploying anything like the number of conventional military forces we sent there in 1990–1991.

Our initiating the use of nuclear weapons today in these or less vital situations would be highly questionable, even if our actual point of self-deterrence were greater than one detonation. This is not to suggest that the United States will be paralyzed if it must confront a nuclear-armed adversary. We dealt with cautious firmness with the Soviet Union during crises over Berlin and Cuba. Still, for nonnuclear powers who feel threatened by the United States today there is a premium on obtaining merely one or two nuclear weapons and the means to deliver them. We would, indeed, pause before intervening militarily against such a country. This is a fact of life that cannot be exorcised by not acknowledging it; it is already quite apparent to Third World nations. Note the statement, attributed to an Indian general following the Gulf War in 1991, that anyone planning to fight the United States had better possess a nuclear weapon.

There is, however, a more subtle point here: Our use of a nuclear weapon in confronting a nuclear power would almost certainly incite a nuclear response, whereas employing a conventional weapon might not. Of course, if we were able to destroy 100 percent of the adversary's nuclear weapons in either one swift offensive attack or with defenses it would be a different matter. Counting on either, however, would be very risky. No offensive or defensive weapons system can ever be so unfailingly reliable and accurate that we could be confident of destroying arsenals of hundreds or thousands of weapons on the ground or in flight. Note that we could not even locate all of Iraq's SCUD missiles and various nuclear, chemical, and biological facilities during the Gulf War. In confronting a nuclear-armed adversary, then, a U.S. president would face a choice of four options: employing nonmilitary means and gambling on being able to resolve the problem satisfactorily; intervening with conventional military force and gambling that this would not push the adversary into a nuclear response; intervening with nuclear weapons and gambling on being able to totally blunt any nuclear retaliation; or intervening with nuclear weapons and being prepared to accept nuclear retaliation. Not only are the nuclear alternatives the most risky, they would carry far-reaching implications, such as breaking the fifty-year history of nonuse of nuclear weapons. I believe they would always come in a poor third.

It is tempting, though, to think we could safely initiate the use of nuclear weapons against a nonnuclear opponent. Clearly, there could not be immediate nuclear retaliation. Such an opponent might be cowed into conceding and then getting on with life. The kinds of opponents we would consider as worthy of an attack with nuclear weapons, however, are likely to be fanatics. Such an aggrieved nonnuclear victim might work doggedly to obtain a nuclear capability with which to exact revenge. Alternatively, resorting to terrorism, perhaps with chemical or biological agents, could be a more immediate alternative. Even if we avoided such consequences, we would have to answer to the international community for breaking the taboo on nuclear weapons; spreading radioactive contamination, real or imagined, beyond the country attacked; causing civilian casualties in the targeted country; and applying disproportionate force. In weighing whether to accept these various risks, we would have to ask, "For what purpose?"

One commonly imputed purpose for our initiating the use of nuclear weapons is to deal with tyrants. Many believe we need the threat of maximum force to deter them. Nuclear weapons could, for instance, threaten them personally, even in deep, hardened bunkers. Or they could threaten a particularly important military unit, like Saddam Hussein's Republican Guard, or underground facilities for manufacturing weapons of mass destruction. Threatening might have its value but would be risky because it is doubtful we would ever follow through and use nuclear weapons for such purposes. In part we would be inhibited by moral considerations. Detonating a sizable groundburst weapon on the middle of a major city such as Baghdad, literally to uproot a dictator like Saddam Hussein, would be a disproportionate action to anything but the most egregious provocation. In part, we would be deterred by the unfathomable responsibility for opening a new nuclear Pandora's box.

A frequently discussed reason for threatening the use of nuclear weapons against tyrants is to deter attacks with chemical or biological weapons. Supposedly, the thinly veiled threat of nuclear retaliation by Secretary of State James Baker deterred Saddam Hussein from employing his chemical weapons during the Gulf War. There is a question as to whether Baker intended such a threat, and we will never know for sure what actually inhibited Saddam Hussein. Very significantly, President Bush and his assistant for national security, Brent Scowcroft, have recently revealed that the president had rejected in advance the option of responding with nuclear weapons were there an Iraqi attack on our forces with chemical weapons.[2]

Another superficially appealing use for nuclear weapons against nonnuclear powers is to extricate ourselves from some difficult tactical situation in conventional war. Nuclear weapons are not very useful tactical instruments, however, when you consider their ancillary effects. They may irradiate territory into which your forces want to move; send radioactive fallout back onto your own forces or cities; and disrupt your own, as well as the enemy's, electronic environment. And even in their smaller forms they can easily be overkill, as tactical weapons come in fifteen sizes but all are large (as noted earlier, the smallest we had, a nuclear artillery shell, was the equivalent force of five B-2 bombers fully loaded with conventional bombs). General Colin Powell deprecated tactical nuclear weapons in his memoirs when discussing a plan he directed be prepared for employing them against the Iraqi army during the Gulf War: "The results unnerved me. To do serious damage to just one armored division dispersed in the desert would require a considerable number of small tactical nuclear weapons. I showed this analysis to [Secretary of Defense Dick] Cheney and then had it destroyed. If I had any doubts before about the practicality of nukes [nuclear weapons] on the field of battle, this report clinched them."[3]

General Powell also supported President Bush's removal of almost all of our tactical weapons from deployed positions. In my experience, this aversion to tactical nuclear weapons is shared by most senior military officers, increasingly so since the mid-1980s. Still, specific arguments for using tactical nuclear weapons crop up regularly:

- One would be to defend the Saudi Arabian oil fields if, for instance, the Iraqis invaded Kuwait again and then thrust south. The oil fields are some 200 miles distant from Kuwait. Moving a substantial armored force that distance over a single highway is a logistical feat quite probably beyond Iraqi capabilities. Even if not, Iraqi forces moving across open desert would be very vulnerable to modest air or missile attacks from Saudi or U.S. forces. Assuming the Iraqis would want to take over the Saudi oil fields reasonably intact, they have no alternative to bringing ground forces to the scene. Nuclear attacks, if they had those weapons, would destroy what they seek to control, and although chemical or biological attacks could disrupt Saudi production, they would not give the Iraqis control. The option, then, of holding off the Iraqi ground forces with nonnuclear forces would certainly be preferred by the Saudis, as well as ourselves.
- Another scenario is the U.S. response to a North Korean invasion of South Korea. North Korea has lost its allies and its access to their military technology; it is in desperate straits economically; and its military forces, although large, simply cannot be well trained or supported. There is evidence, for instance, that North Korean Air Force pilots get fewer training hours in the air in one year than ours do in one month. Senior U.S. military officers do not question that we and the South Koreans could defeat such an invasion by North Korean conventional forces without resort to nuclear weapons. Nor could resort to chemical or biological warfare give North Korea more than a temporary advantage. Such an attack would have to concentrate on Seoul and/or on the mass

of U.S. and South Korean forces along the demilitarized zone between the countries. It could be very damaging, but there are sufficient U.S. forces elsewhere in South Korea, in Japan, and at sea to overwhelm North Korea quickly. The fact that we have withdrawn all nuclear weapons from South Korea, although they could be returned quickly, indicates that we do not see defense of South Korea as a vital use for these weapons.

- Still another possibility would be to conduct preemptive nuclear attacks to prevent the further proliferation of chemical, biological, and nuclear weapons. A problem here is whether our own public, let alone the world community, could be persuaded this was justified. Could we present conclusive intelligence that what was going on, indeed, was the manufacture of weapons of mass destruction? And even if we could, would there be enough to be gained to warrant unleashing the nuclear genie?
- Another possibility is a Russian invasion of its neighbors, such as Poland and Ukraine; or a Chinese invasion of its neighbors, such as Korea, Taiwan, and Japan. In any of these circumstances, the overriding consideration would be whether we would risk general nuclear war and the survival of our own society on behalf of those countries. If so, where would we stop short of becoming the world's nuclear policeman?

Another factor to consider is that we possess the most powerful conventional military forces in the world—an advantage that will likely continue for the foreseeable future. No other conventional military force comes close to ours in sophistication, both in equipment and in battlefield techniques. Moreover, no other force is as well trained to fight and logistically prepared to do so. If there are military challenges we cannot meet with U.S. conventional forces, they are at the low end of the spectrum, like jungle or urban warfare or terrorism. Nuclear weapons would hardly be applicable. There should, for the foreseeable future, be little reason to let ourselves get into situations where the use of nuclear weapons could seem to be important militarily. It would be very difficult to explain to our own public, let alone the world, that we could not find some nonnuclear alternative. We would have to face the accusation that we had been seduced into leaning on our nuclear strength as a less expensive alternative, as with NATO in 1952.

We have downgraded tactical nuclear weapons in recent years, despite the fact that these smaller ones would likely be the weapon of choice if we were ever to initiate the use of nuclear weapons. In 1991 we unilaterally withdrew all but a few hundred of them from bases in Europe and from all naval ships. Beyond that, we are voluntarily dismantling many tactical warheads, even before strategic ones.

Any nuclear power must consider the point at which it is self-deterred. It is often suggested that a "mad Russian" might be willing to accept more damage in retaliation than we would consider reasonable, as is evidenced by Russia's historical perseverance in responding to invasions. Persevering, though, is different from taking a positive decision to accept the risks of heavy losses as a result of initiating nuclear war. And with the Soviet Union having collapsed in good measure because of economic insufficiency, Russians know they need to build economic strength rather than subject themselves to the possibility of nuclear destruction. To estimate the points of self-deterrence as one detonation for the United States and hundreds or even thousands for Russia is illogical. Since the end of the Cold War there is growing evidence that Soviet leaders were quite realistic in understanding the unacceptability of nuclear damage. For instance, during a conversation I had in 1990 with the Soviet Union's former top military officer, Marshal Sergei Akhromeyev, he made it clear he was under no illusions as to the utility of these weapons.*

It is difficult to estimate China's point of self-deterrence, just as with its point of non-recovery. We simply know less of its leaders' views on nuclear matters, because we have not had the kinds of discussions with them we have with the Russians. Nor do we understand the psychology of having a population of more than 1 billion people. China, though, has much to lose in a nuclear war. Although its economic output per capita is only one-tenth that of the United States, China's economy is growing at a rate close to 10 percent per annum. It is hard to imagine that the Chinese leadership would jeopardize that success by risking nuclear damage. Thus, China's point of self-deterrence may not be significantly different from those of other large countries.

---

*My conversation with Marshal Akhromeyev is discussed in Chapter 5.

As for smaller nations that may become nuclear powers, points of self-deterrence will be very low, since only a small number of nuclear detonations would push them past their points of non-recovery. The issue is whether any leader would be so fanatic as to accept considerable nuclear destruction in order to achieve some objective. Even fanatic leaders, if rational, must make a calculation of net benefits. If they anticipate a response that would push their country past its point of non-recovery, it is difficult to believe they would decide to use nuclear weapons. If leaders are irrational, there is no way to deter them from irrational acts, other than hoping that within their regime there will be others who will effect restraint. However, different values, rather than irrationality, may lead some leaders to stress some values, often religious or political, more than others. This, or a miscalculation, could lead to the use of nuclear weapons. It would likely be because a strong psychic benefit, such as an Arab state seeking to destroy Israel, overrode a rational estimate of the probability and extent of the likely retaliation. Thus, whereas the point of self-deterrence is logically low for such states, in some cases it may not be so in practice because the risks are not sufficiently clear.

There are also self-deterring forces working on terrorists. One is that the odiousness of a nuclear detonation could boomerang and lose them support were they identified with it. Also, an actual nuclear detonation would likely be overkill for their purposes. Still, because threatening a nuclear explosion in a major city has to be the ultimate in extortion, we cannot count on self-deterrence here.

From nuclear powers to terrorist groups, then, the very power of nuclear weapons restrains their use. The cause of this restraint ranges from the risk of retaliation in kind, to the uncertainty involved with breaking the more than fifty-year taboo on the use of these weapons, to the likelihood any use will be seen as a disproportionate response to anything but a nuclear attack. With respect to chemical and biological weapons, it is not the potency but the widespread sense of odiousness of their use that is self-deterring. This is reflected in the fact that many nations have voluntarily forsworn their possession and use through signing the Chemical and Biological Weapons Conventions. Yet there are nations that have not signed the Conventions, and there are those who have but may be hedging their bets by retaining and developing these weapons.

As shown in Table 3.1, thirteen nations that might want chemical or biological weapons and have the technical capability to manage them have not signed the CWC; sixteen have not signed the BWC. We are confident that five nations possess chemical programs, all except Iraq being signatories to the CWC (one, the United States, is fully committed to disbanding its chemical weapons); we suspect another seventeen have them also. As to biological programs, we know that two countries have them and suspect fourteen more. All told, that results in concern for thirty-five nations on the chemical side and thirty-two on the biological. Why is there this much interest in these weapons, some of it duplicitous?

As far as nuclear powers are concerned, as we have seen, it is unlikely any one would employ chemical or biological weapons against another, since nuclear weapons would be so much more effective. They could, though, utilize them to punish a lesser power, even to push one to a point of non-recovery. This, for instance, might appear appropriate in response to a chemical or biological attack and preferable to escalating to nuclear weapons. Still, breaking the taboo on these weapons would be seen and treated as being irresponsible. That would especially be the case since all of the nuclear powers have signed the CWC and the BWC, with the exception of Israel on the latter. It is one thing for a nation like Iraq to break the taboo, quite another for a major world power. Overall, chemical and biological weapons have a sufficiently negative stigma that they are unlikely to be the preferred weapon for major powers against lesser powers. Because of the dire condition of Russia's conventional military forces today, however, we cannot rule out Russia's resort to chemical or biological weapons if militarily hard-pressed by some smaller yet troublesome power. In such a case chemical weapons would be the more likely choice, as there is at least some precedent for their use.

Thus, smaller military powers are the most likely to employ chemical and biological weapons. One perceived reason would be to offset the superior conventional forces of a major power. A smaller power might expect that the threat of chemical or biological attack would deter a major power from intervening. Iraq might well have hoped this would be the case after its invasion of Kuwait in 1990. A smaller power engaged militarily with a major one might also resort to actual use to offset the major power's superiority. The Department of Defense commissioned a study in 1997 on how chemical or biological attacks could be employed to disrupt

TABLE 3.1 Known and Suspected Activity in Chemical and Biological Weaponry

	Chemical	*Biological*
Significant nations that have not signed the International Convention[a]	Angola Botswana Egypt Eritrea Iraq North Korea Lebanon Libya Mozambique Serbia and Montenegro Somalia Sudan Syria	Algeria Angola Azerbaijan Cameroon Chad Eritrea Guinea Israel Kazakhstan Kyrgyzstan Lithuania Mauritania Moldova Namibia Tajikistan Zambia
Nations known to have programs	India Iraq Russia South Korea U.S.	Iraq Russia
Nations suspected of having programs	Bulgaria China Cuba Czech Republic Egypt Iran Israel Libya North Korea Pakistan Romania Saudi Arabia South Africa South Korea Syria Taiwan[b] Vietnam	China Cuba Egypt India Iran Israel Libya North Korea Pakistan South Africa South Korea Syria Taiwan[b]

NOTES: [a]In weaning down to "significant" the following smaller nations have been excluded on the grounds that they are unlikely to have either the desire or the capability for producing biological or chemical weapons: Andorra, Antigua and Barbuda, Barbados, Belize, Comoros, Djibouti, French Guiana, Kiribati, Marshall Islands, Micronesia, Monaco, Nauru, Niue, Palau, Puerto Rico, Saint Vincent and the Grenadines, Sao Tome and Principe, Solomon Islands, Swaziland, Tonga, Trinidad and Tobago, Tuvalu, Vanuatu, Western Samoa.
[b] Taiwan, no longer being recognized by the United Nations, is unable to sign the CWC or BWC.

the dispatch of U.S. forces overseas.[4] The objective would be to delay the arrival of those forces until an aggressive action was a fait accompli. The study hypothesized contaminating chemical or biological attacks on ports of embarkation in the United States and those of debarkation for U.S. forces overseas. It is a feasible scenario, though an improbable one because it requires such a sophisticated, precision effort, with much of it carried out by a foreign power inside the United States. Moreover, the attacking nation would be exposed to immediate retaliation by other U.S. forces not affected, such as long-range bombers and aircraft carriers. Still, major powers will not be able to engage smaller ones without taking precautions against chemical and biological attacks.

Accordingly, smaller powers are much more likely to be tempted to use chemical or biological weapons against major powers using surreptitious attacks, hoping to avoid retaliation. This would be state-supported terrorism more than warfare. The defining issues would be how capable a smaller power could be in manufacturing sophisticated chemical or biological agents and how effectively it could deliver them. Whether delivery of aerosols could be surreptitious depends on the scale. A single truck or crop duster could spray a great deal of vapor. With the proper agent, either method could result in thousands or even hundreds of thousands of fatalities. If this were carried out on a national scale, it is highly doubtful the culprits could avoid being identified. There is no doubt, however, that all societies are vulnerable.

Terrorist groups, in contrast to small nations, could feel less threatened by retaliation because they can be more difficult to identify and are less vulnerable to retaliation, as they have no territory per se to defend. Unfortunately, terrorist groups are showing signs of increasing interest in biological and chemical agents. Japan's Aum Shinrikyo is one example. Its attack in the Tokyo subway with sarin gas killed only twelve people because it was clumsy. Not only could such a chemical attack have been more lethal, biological agents carry even more damaging potential. There is, however, disagreement as to the probability that terrorists will use biological weapons. Manufacturing them is inexpensive and relatively easy. The quantities needed to spread harm are small and, hence, readily transportable for clandestine infiltration. Yet containing the lethal microorganisms and toxins during manufacturing is by no means simple. As has been noted, stabilizing the agent can require expensive, complex technologies beyond the reach of many countries, let alone terrorist groups. And delivery is an additional, complex technological obstacle. A common fallacy is that biological (or chemical) agents could merely be dropped into a city's water reservoir. The dilution factor, plus the effect of water chlorination, are more than enough to defeat these agents. Added together, the requirements for using biological agents are much more demanding than those for chemical agents. A common view—one I share—is that terrorists would prefer chemical agents.

Chemical and biological weapons might also be used by one smaller military power against other smaller military powers. The example of the tactical military advantages Iraq gained over Iran during 1986–1988 must encourage other modest military powers to look in the direction of chemical weapons for use on the battlefield. And even though chemical and biological attacks are unlikely to drive sizable nations, like the United States, to non-recovery, that might not be the case with countries whose populations are much smaller. It is noteworthy, however, that during modern times most actual chemical attacks have been against unprotected citizens or troops; we have yet to see how effective defenses may become against chemical and biological warfare.

Finally, and unfortunately, we also need to acknowledge the possibility of fanatic leaders using chemical and biological agents against dissident elements of their own populations. The Iraqis again set the example with chemical attacks on Kurds and Shiites during 1987.

As far as the United States is concerned, the larger threat from chemical and biological agents is in limited, covert attacks by terrorists or smaller powers. These could be local disasters, though not nation-threatening. Why, then, is Russia known to have hidden biological and chemical programs and China suspected of having them? The most probable explanation is that they do not want to be left behind should a technical breakthrough turn these into highly effective weapons. Another reason could be the traditional belief that to deter the use of nuclear, biological, and chemical weapons a country needs to possess such weapons itself. We need to convince them that deterrence is a function of threatening unacceptable damage, not damage in kind; matching weapons is not essential to deterrence.

The world community has made strong statements that chemical and biological weapons are unacceptable for either possession or use. The issue before us is whether the world community can neutralize these weapons by strengthening the historical abhorrence of them.

4

CONTROLLED RESPONSE

IN JANUARY 1977, I WAS INVITED to a meeting of the Conference Board, a group of business leaders that gathers periodically to discuss business issues. I was impressed with how knowledgeable and interested they also were on issues of national security. Obviously, they had brought in a military officer like myself because of that interest.

Surprisingly, I found considerable concern on their part as to the balance of U.S.-Soviet nuclear forces. They asked whether we were as far behind the Soviets as many feared. Did we need a larger ICBM to match the ones the Soviets had? Did not those large Soviet missiles make us vulnerable to a surprise attack? And did the Soviets' extensive program of civil defense shelters make them less vulnerable to our retaliation if they should attack us first?

It particularly intrigued me that business leaders would be so informed on a subject as out of the ordinary as civil defense. I had always been skeptical of civil defense programs. We had all seen that President Kennedy's effort to induce us to build home shelters and to vitalize a broad program of preparations for nuclear attack had failed. I had seen very little secret data on the Soviets' program but sensed that what I was hearing was exaggerated.

Within two months of this meeting, I unexpectedly became Director of Central Intelligence. One of my early objectives was to make the CIA more open to the American public. The agency had just been through a series of investigations—with resulting widespread criticism. It needed to show Americans more of what it was doing on their behalf, within the limits of secrecy, of course. My plan was to produce more unclassified analyses on topics of interest to the public. Searching for a suitable topic for the trial run of this new policy, I recalled the Conference Board meeting and decided the issue would be Soviet civil defense.

It took time to persuade the professionals in CIA that it was a reasonable idea. The result, however, was revealing: On an unclassified basis we could say that only 10–20 percent of the urban population of the Soviet Union could be sheltered; primary reliance was on the evacuation of cities.[1] This was almost a charade. If the United States were to strike first, there would be no time for evacuation. If the Soviets were to strike first, they could not risk moving streams of people out of their major cities in advance and thereby tipping their hand. Moreover, during winter, evacuation would be unfeasible in places like Moscow. Protecting 20 percent in shelters might be nice for the leadership if there were a nuclear war, but what kind of a country would they have left to lead? Even if no Soviets were killed, where would the people go and what would they do when they returned from evacuation or came out of their shelters into devastated cities? There would be nothing much left.

The evidence was there, however, that the Soviets were spending money and building shelters. On the one hand, it was futile and wasteful. On the other, it was a government doing what it could in case deterrence failed.

ALTHOUGH WE HOPE WE CAN DETER INDEFINITELY all use of weapons of mass destruction, we need to think through what our response would be to varying types of attacks with them, starting with the worst (although least likely): a major nuclear attack that pushed the United States past non-recovery. Only Russia is currently capable of inflicting such damage, but we would have only one option in responding: Having little left to lose and not wanting the Russian aggression to pay off, we would have to attempt to push Russia past its point of non-recovery, presumably with our nuclear weapons. That means we must study what that would require, that is, what Russia's point of non-recovery is. Neither side, of course, would win. Hence, it is difficult to imagine what would lead the Russians to pursue such self-defeating aggression.

Some experts have argued that we would be deterred from launching any counterattack at all because doing so would invite even more destruction on the United States, that is, we would be pushed even beyond non-recovery. This argument typifies one of the problems we have long had with constructing nuclear strategy. It assumes we would be capable of precisely calculated responses amid an unimaginable calamity to our society. This would not be like losing a battle and regrouping to fight on; it would be losing a society including certainly tens of millions of people, then trying to survive. Who could possibly predict how we would react? We cannot even forecast who would be around to make decisions for the nation—or whether those in authority could control our surviving nuclear forces well enough to strike back. In short, we have developed nuclear strategies as though we were playing chess, without considering both the emotional and practical stresses induced by widespread nuclear destruction. What our next move would be after being pushed past our point of non-recovery is simply unpredictable.

Ironically, other strategists have argued that in the event of an attack pushing us past non-recovery we must be prepared not only to push Russia past non-recovery in return but also to attack every remaining Russian weapon of mass destruction so as to minimize further damage to ourselves. This argument reveals yet another flaw in our strategic decision process: preparing for any possible contingency, no matter how slight the probability of doing any good. In this case, most of Russia's nuclear arsenal would already have been launched, and the remainder would be on alert to launch out from any incoming attack.

We need to think also about responding to lesser aggressions, from a single nuclear warhead to a relatively "modest" number. There could be attacks on the United States or other countries, including attacks on U.S. forces overseas. There are a number of scenarios for such limited attacks.

Pure accident could be one. As noted earlier, we have had eleven accidents in which nuclear weapons were lost from U.S. aircraft and a number involving submarines loaded with nuclear weapons. The safety features that we built into the weapons prevented any detonations. We understand that the Soviet, and now the Russian, safety arrangements are similar. Today, however, the startling deterioration of Russia's military plant, including nuclear-powered submarines rusting at their piers, forces us to wonder how well these precautions are being observed. And the ongoing demoralization of Russia's military personnel has created the risk of mistakes during training exercises that could result in the unintended launching of nuclear weapons. As far as the other existing nuclear powers, we

know rather little of their accident records. Clearly, their military establishments can have accidents, just as we.

A second cause of a limited attack could be from miscalculation. The
United States has gone to nuclear alert more than 1,500 times without
cause.[2] The chances of such incidents resulting in the unintended launch
of a nuclear weapon have been low, in good part because we have always
been skeptical of the evidence of an impending attack and in part because
we understood the Soviets or Russians knew that neither of us could win
by initiating nuclear war. But those calming ingredients might not exist
between other national rivals. This is precisely what is so alarming about
having India and Pakistan move closer to a ready nuclear posture. Here
are two countries with a long-standing and heated rivalry; with a common, disputed border; and with little experience in, or equipment for, exercising positive command over nuclear weapons.

A third cause could be the unauthorized use of nuclear weapons. The
United States has taken extensive precautions to prevent this. In some of
our weapons systems, two keys must be turned nearly simultaneously to
launch a nuclear weapon, and wherever feasible the keys are physically
separated so that one person could not turn both. In others there is an
electronic locking system whereby a coded message must be received and
inserted into the locking device to unlock it. Still, it is difficult not to believe that such controls could not, with some ingenuity, be bypassed. Our
real protection is confidence in our personnel, that is, the low probability
that enough people would deliberately try to circumvent the rules to
make it possible to do so. That might not hold up, however, if there was
consensus among personnel that communications with superior authorities had broken down and releasing nuclear weapons quickly was vital to
the survival of the United States. Russia has had similar, perhaps even
more secure, systems of control over the release of nuclear weapons. But
again, we must question whether these will be enough if Russia's military
and political vicissitudes continue. British and French control systems appear to approximate ours. We know rather little about China's and less
about those of Israel, Pakistan, and India. What is most worrying, however, is whether rogue states that acquire these weapons would establish
good controls. On the one hand, dictators are wont to retain a firm hand
over their military. On the other hand, there are greater risks of fanatics in
the military establishments of rogue states. One specter is that of a group

of extremist Arab officers feeling justified in launching a nuclear weapon at Israel; another is fanatics from any nation with deep, historical rivalries wanting to take advantage of a newfound nuclear edge.

And finally there is the chance for deliberate use. In my opinion, it is inconceivable that the United States, Britain, or France would initiate nuclear war. Historically, Russia and China have not been inclined to do so, either. We cannot rule that out, however, in light of the uncertainties as to the types of leadership and political structures those two countries will develop in the future. India, Pakistan, and Israel could be tempted to employ nuclear weapons in self-defense against a conventional assault that threatened their survival, although Pakistan and India would have to consider that their opponents, India and China, respectively, are more heavily armed nuclear powers.

In sum, with the existing nuclear powers there will always be some risk of the use of nuclear weapons. Short of major changes in the world's political climate, this is a low probability, with the possible exception of India and Pakistan. But what of new nuclear powers? A principal concern is that one of the rogue states might obtain a nuclear capability before its rival and attack while it had that advantage. We also must be concerned that fanatics could attack anyone, including larger nuclear powers. Some leader with a nuclear weapon might find a psychic satisfaction in damaging Israel, or Russia, or China, or the Great Satan of the United States that would offset any retaliation by the victim. Fanatics might also miscalculate the resolve of the nation being attacked and expect to avoid any retaliation, or they might believe they could disguise their attack and escape undetected. In sum, we would consider a fanatic's attack on a major nuclear power as irrational, but it certainly cannot be ruled out. Terrorists are another matter, since they have no territory to speak of that is vulnerable to counterattack. Fortunately, as far as we know, terrorists have not demonstrated serious interest in obtaining nuclear devices. Still, the planting and detonating of crude nuclear devices by terrorists cannot be ruled out.

The normal maxims of warfare are not applicable in the context of limited nuclear attacks. In thinking through how to respond, we face the dilemma of needing to use military force while suppressing the normal military instinct to use it as forcefully as capabilities permit. In military jargon the standard objective in warfare is to establish a "favorable exchange ratio," that is, if your opponent does one unit of damage to you, you must do two or three to him. Theoretically, that should wear down your opponent's will to continue. A favorable exchange ratio does not guarantee victory, but military leaders will almost always seek one. For instance, when the 1994 Nuclear Posture Review called for our retaining 10,000 nuclear warheads rather than 3,500, it was presumably to ensure we would never be at an unfavorable exchange ratio with the Russians. The problem is that in achieving a favorable ratio we would also bring more unacceptable damage on ourselves in retaliation.

One precaution would be to ensure that we do not panic when facing nuclear detonations or the spread of chemical and biological agents. During the past fifty years we have come too close to mistakes and accidents as a result of being on hair-trigger alert. Thus, it is essential that we have nuclear retaliatory forces that are so secure that we need not fear their destruction before we can use them. There are two approaches to invulnerability: numbers and stealth. During the 1940s and 1950s, we turned to numbers of bombers. Since the early 1960s, we have relied on numbers of ICBMs and bombers and on stealth in submarines. Today, as both we and the Russians reduce numbers through mutual agreement, we are implicitly rejecting security in numbers. The ICBM does not have many other virtues. Even worse, it has the major disadvantage of making it appear that we intend to take the offense. We deny that, but anyone sitting in a vulnerable ICBM silo understands that firing first will very likely be necessary to achieving the mission. Another disadvantage is that the sense of vulnerability of ICBMs has prompted us to adopt the risky procedures of high alert, such as being ready to launch thousands of missiles with only a few minutes' warning. However, the ICBM is not nearly as vulnerable as our precautions suggest. The probability of Russia being able to coordinate a perfect, near-simultaneous attack on even a modest force of ICBMs is very low. Enough of them would surely survive that the Russians would be self-deterred. The ICBM, then, is a liability because it carries an image of vulnerability more than an actual vulnerability. That image drives us to large numbers and to risky readiness procedures. Those make it appear we favor taking the offense.

The second most vulnerable element of our nuclear retaliatory forces is the bomber leg. Bombers, however, can be moved among bases and even launched as a precaution and then recalled. Thus, they are less of a liability than ICBMs. As a practical matter, our country is going to maintain a force of high-performance bombers for conventional missions. The marginal cost of retaining some of them in a dual nuclear role would be small.

The least vulnerable retaliatory forces by far are the Navy's strategic ballistic missile submarines. Their disadvantages are that they are expensive and that they carry a large number of warheads in one platform (192 at full load). We could ameliorate costs by shifting some of the burden of invulnerability to the Navy's force of attack submarines (SSNs). In a mix of SSBNs with sea-launched ballistic missiles and SSNs with sea-launched cruise missiles (SLCMs), the attack submarines would be virtually free of cost because the Navy expects to maintain forty to fifty SSNs for conventional warfare anyway. A few cruise missiles could be accommodated in some or all of them without serious penalty. These cruise missiles would also be a hedge against an effective antiballistic missile defense system because they are air-breathing rather than ballistic.

There are two solutions to having too many warheads in one submarine platform: (1) decrease the number of warheads per submarine and increase the number of submarines at additional cost; or (2) spread sea-based retaliatory capability across both types of submarines. Having more platforms is also a hedge against a breakthrough in submarine detection techniques, although concern over this has been considerably overplayed. In the extreme, even if submerged submarines were to become fully visible, they would still be less vulnerable than fixed ICBMs, which are not only visible but do not move. Submarines are likely to become more visible in time, but a breakthrough to full visibility is unlikely. We and the Russians have dedicated immense efforts for more than fifty years to detecting submarines, and almost every gain has been offset by countermeasures. Moreover, detection of a single submarine is only the beginning. A nuclear aggressor would have to count on being able to knock out an entire force of submarines before any one of them could launch retaliatory attacks. Such nearly simultaneous actions would be a formidable task. Thus, although we should not ignore the possibility of increased vulnerability of submarines, the precaution of backing them up with even more vulnerable ICBMs has never made sense.

Dispensing with ICBMs as numbers of weapons decrease overall is inevitable; even many within the Air Force would agree. Yet it will be difficult politically to tip the balance of strategic nuclear forces decidedly toward the

Navy, that is, to place most of our strategic retaliatory forces in SSBNs and SSNs. Somehow we will have to break the enshrined concept of the TRIAD of strategic forces consisting of ICBMs, bombers, and SSBNs. More than one system is desirable, but there is no magic in three or of these particular ones: The most desirable mix—bombers, SSBNs, and SSNs—happens to be a TRIAD also. It would give us the best assurance we need of being able to retaliate against any nuclear aggression without panic.

The next question is how we should react if deterrence does fail. With respect to a nuclear attack, there are three options: (1) not respond; (2) respond at or above the level of destruction of the aggression; and (3) respond at a lower level:

- Not to respond. This would invite more nuclear aggression; for a very small or perhaps accidental attack, however, it could serve as a prudent brake on escalation.
- To respond by exchanging blows until one side capitulates. This would invite more nuclear destruction on the United States, regardless of whether we "won" by doing more total damage to the opponent. The exception to this is the unlikely event that our retaliation completely disarmed the aggressor's remaining nuclear capability.
- To respond at a lower level, rather than escalate. This might encourage the aggressor to call a halt to the use of nuclear weapons and attempt to resolve differences by other means before matters got out of hand. McGeorge Bundy, in his landmark book on nuclear policy, favored what he termed the "less-than-equal reply." He pointed out that "there is a compelling difference between having a survivable capacity for destruction, and a decision to inflict that destruction after deterrence has failed."[3]

There are unconventional ways to respond to limited nuclear attacks with "less-than-equal" forcefulness:

- Attacks on a number of the aggressor's most valuable facilities, governmental and industrial, could be made with nuclear weapons delivery systems carrying dummies (e.g., lead weights instead of warheads). Dropping several of these into the Kremlin, for instance, would do limited damage but send an unmistakable signal as to what could come next. We would, of course, have to design and manufacture these special warheads and have them ready to mount.

- High-altitude nuclear bursts designed to produce EMPs could be directed at urban-industrial areas. These could temporarily knock out industrial operations, with no other physical destruction and only limited deaths due to outages of electricity. These bursts could be sustained for periods of time to reinforce the message as to how vulnerable the aggressor's society is. The psychological impact alone could be considerable. Again, this is an option that would require advance design, production, and operational planning. For instance, in order to avoid unwanted electronic effects on our satellites in space, we would need to install special shielding on the upper hemisphere of the weapon and calculate the combination of weapon yield and altitude of burst that would minimize energy escaping into space.
- Precision attacks with conventional or nuclear weapons could be made on a sizable number of important industrial facilities, such as power plants and key points in communications and transportation systems. These would minimize deaths but indicate how fragile the aggressor's industrial structure is.
- Any of these limited responses could be misinterpreted by the aggressor and trigger further attacks. To avoid this we would want to attempt to communicate to the aggressor that we were launching a limited response and that it would be a good idea to ride it out and then negotiate.

These kinds of options for retaliating to a limited nuclear attack could be called a *doctrine of controlled response*. Just how "controlled" these responses became would be a function of the nature of the nuclear aggression and the psychology of the aggressor. For instance, in the case of a limited attack by Russia on the United States, we would select controlled options against the Russian homeland. If the attack were against U.S. forces overseas, we might use options against Russian military forces either at home or abroad. For limited nuclear attacks by smaller countries, either on the United States or U.S. forces overseas, controlled response options like EMP bursts could be particularly appropriate, for a single burst could easily blanket many countries. In the case of clandestine nuclear attacks on the United States by either an unidentified small nuclear power or a terrorist group, nonlethal or minimally lethal controlled responses on the primary suspects could be an alternative to doing nothing.

Perhaps the most cogent objection to the doctrine of controlled response is that simply discussing less than fully lethal responses to a nuclear attack weakens our deterrent threat. It is an axiom of conventional war that deterrence is a function of both military power and the will to apply that power. In other words, possessing force alone will not deter your adversary if it appears you do not have the will to employ that force. However, this axiom is not applicable in the context of nuclear deterrence. Any nation considering aggression against the United States could not help recognizing that our overwhelming capabilities with nuclear weapons could end their society. To gamble that we did not have the will to use it, no matter what our stated policy, would be an enormous risk. In short, when the force is immense, the factor of will does not have a significant impact on the product.

How likely is it that a controlled response would induce an opponent not only to cease nuclear aggression but to capitulate by making reparations and opening its nuclear establishment to international supervision? An aggressor, knowing that ultimately we have greater power, would either have been desperate or have made a tremendous miscalculation. It is possible, then, that a controlled response could provide a much-needed opportunity for the aggressor to reassess matters. Controlled response is not something a president could decide on easily, because there would be public pressure to punish any nuclear aggressor severely, and there is good reason to question whether a controlled response would accomplish all we would need to accomplish. Still, the alternatives are not attractive, and we need not rush into war-fighting if we have invulnerable retaliatory forces (e.g., SSBNs and SSNs). We could attempt controlled response without losing the option of responding more forcefully later on.

The three major concepts discussed thus far—*point of non-recovery, point of self-deterrence*, and *controlled response*—together offer a new theoretical foundation for our nuclear strategy. The old strategy, whatever its merits in its day, led us to produce inordinate numbers of these weapons, a willingness to accept great risks in maintaining weapons in conditions of high alert, and war plans that reached such astronomical lengths that no individual could comprehend them. Not many of those who wrote those million pages of war plans believed they would work. Not many who organized the alert procedures believed such plans were wise. Not many who did the analyses that proved we needed 32,500 nuclear warheads believed in anything close to that number. And not many who estimated the extent of probable damage in our war plans believed the United States and Russia could survive the consequences of a nuclear exchange. Some played these games for the intellectual challenge; some played to enhance the parochial interests of a military service or an industry. The more serious and intelligent participated in making these plans because they believed the only way to deter nuclear war was to have the plans and the capabilities to carry them out.

With the end of the Cold War, our sizable edge in economic, political, and military power places us in a favorable position to question whether we need to go to such extremes in order to deter convincingly. During the Cold War, with a sense of imminent threat, it would have been difficult to change strategies that, although risky, were working. Today, we can afford to experiment with more consistent premises and then attempt to lead the other nuclear powers into adopting them. Russia's economic plight will make it difficult for it to resist our lead. The British and the French might resist changes in nuclear doctrine, but intensive consultations should bring them along. China's response would be difficult to predict, but it has never adopted some of our most pernicious theories, such as the importance of nuclear parity and the advantages of initiating nuclear war. The time is ripe, then, to discard many of the past premises of our nuclear strategy. Doing so would open new possibilities for nuclear stability.

As for aggression with chemical and biological weapons, our decisions on how to respond are simplified by the fact that the United States has eschewed any use of biological and chemical weapons both through unilateral pronouncement and through adherence to the CWC and BWC. Beyond that, we have no biological weapons today, and by 2007 we should have no chemical weapons. Thus, we can rule out responding to biological and chemical attacks in kind. The issue of response is complicated, however, by frequent statements by U.S. government officials that we retain the option of responding to chemical and biological attacks with nuclear weapons and that such a threat is the key to deterring these attacks in the first place. That thesis raises three issues we must think through: Should we plan to use nuclear weapons in response to biological and chemical attacks? Would we actually use them if we were attacked? And should we threaten their use, whether we would actually use them or not?

The strongest argument for responding to chemical and biological attacks with nuclear weapons is that doing so is the best deterrent to further use by the aggressor. It would also help dissuade others who might be tempted to use them. The next strongest argument in favor of nuclear retaliation is that employing chemical and biological weapons is universally seen as an egregious act and deserves a very strong response. And, finally, if we had threatened nuclear retaliation, we would undermine all future deterrence if we did not follow through. The key argument against a nuclear response to biological and chemical attacks is that it is difficult to find suitable targets for nuclear weapons. We have had the real-life example of the Gulf War in 1991 where, as noted earlier, President Bush looked at the idea of a nuclear response to chemical attacks and rejected it. As also noted earlier, General Powell looked at using tactical nuclear weapons on military targets during that same war. He found, though, that the destruction of a single Iraqi division would require an inordinate number of them. We could have attacked Iraqi industry instead. That would likely have led us to the oil fields centered on Kirkuk. These are the key economic assets of Iraq and are distant from major population centers. Would we, though, want to disable Iraq's primary source of income and deprive the world oil market of Iraqi production? In still another option, we could have attacked Baghdad with one or several sizable nuclear weapons to burrow into Saddam Hussein's underground bunkers or just to attack the city and its industry. In either event, the result would have been massive loss of life.

The dilemma here is to find targets that are of sufficient value to be an adequate retribution, but not so damaging as to be disproportionate to the provocation. Any of the above options would almost certainly have been seen as disproportionate to a chemical attack. It is almost as certain they would also have been seen as disproportionate with a biological one, unless that attack was exceptionally lethal. Any response with nuclear weapons would likely also have aroused resentment in neighboring states threatened by radioactivity, in the Arab world in general, and by nations around the world who want to maintain the taboo on the use of nuclear weapons.

In the longer term, one disadvantage of a nuclear response to chemical and biological attacks would be the impact on our efforts to prevent the proliferation of nuclear weapons. If we need them for this purpose, how can we tell would-be proliferators such as North Korea, Iraq, and Iran that they might not find them useful also?

These advantages and disadvantages need to be weighed against the alternatives, the most obvious of which is massive use of conventional force. We certainly have superior conventional military capabilities. The weakness of relying on retaliation with conventional force is the time it might take to arrive on the scene and do the job. We can, with foresight, build conventional forces that emphasize mobility. Planning to rely on nuclear weapons, however, could lead to neglect of the conventional alternative.

The second issue is whether we actually *would* use nuclear weapons in response to chemical and biological attacks. This is different from whether we *should*. I believe President Bush's rejection of the nuclear alternative reflects the immense responsibility any U.S. president must feel with respect to unleashing the nuclear genie again. At the same time, however, we must recognize that the American public could become so outraged at any use of biological and chemical agents as to demand the strongest possible response. In our democracy we cannot predict public reaction with assurance and its effect on policymakers. Consequently, the threat of a nuclear response will always be there. No opponent could afford to ignore that possibility because the risks of misjudging our reaction are too high. This approach to being able to threaten without threatening is termed *existential deterrence*. It may appear to be hypocrisy, but it is simply a statement of fact that nuclear powers threaten no matter what they pledge. Relying on existential deterrence would only be hypocritical if we were absolutely convinced in advance that we would resort to nuclear weapons. Only a president could make that judgment; considering that no president has taken that option for more than a half-century, none are likely to take such a resolute position in advance.

Besides relying on existential deterrence, there is another good reason not to threaten nuclear response directly: There exists the high probability that we would not follow through and actually use those weapons, particularly against a chemical attack or a limited biological one. In that case, the credibility of our future efforts to deter would be suspect.

In sum, on the three points in question:

- We should not plan to use nuclear weapons in response to chemical and biological attacks because it is too likely to be disproportionate.
- We would actually use nuclear weapons in response to biological and chemical attacks only in the case of the most egregious biological attack.
- We need not threaten a nuclear response to biological and chemical attacks in order to deter them.

We also need to address in advance what an appropriate response would be to chemical and biological attacks against a target other than the United States and its forces overseas. Having for many years assured our allies we would come to their aid in the event of a nuclear attack against them, we are almost obliged to include attacks by these other weapons of mass destruction. It seems very unlikely we would resort to nuclear weapons for that purpose, other than in the most egregious of cases. The United States, though, clearly has selfish, as well as unselfish, reasons for wanting to arrest any use of weapons of mass destruction. How far we would go to punish an aggressor who employed a weapon of mass destruction against others would depend on whether we had built such an international consensus against the use of weapons of mass destruction that adequate collective, international punishment could be administered instead to deter further use.

Part Three

The Solution

5

STRATEGIC ESCROW

IN OCTOBER 1990, I visited Moscow as a private citizen, a tourist. I did, however, request a meeting with Marshal Sergei Akhromeyev, former chief of the Soviet general staff and at the time a key adviser to President Mikhail Gorbachev. At 8:00 P.M. one evening a black limousine picked me up at my hotel and drove me through a towered gate into the courtyard of the Kremlin. I was escorted up a broad staircase and down a long, empty corridor with lots of doors but no decoration. The room I was ushered into was sparse as well, with only a modest bare table, a few chairs, and a map of the world on one wall.

In a few moments the marshal, a slim, balding man in a uniform sporting myriad decorations, came in. His eyes were penetrating, but he exuded friendliness. It was to be just the two of us and an interpreter. As fellow military men, we quickly found grounds for discussion. He started by berating me for the threat our Navy's aircraft carriers posed to his country. I replied that those carriers were useful in many places, but we would never risk sending them close enough to the Soviet Union in wartime to be a serious threat.

I then took my turn to suggest that we both knew our countries had far too many nuclear weapons. Akhromeyev flashed an instant *Da!* almost before the translator stopped. I next suggested he persuade President Gorbachev to dispose unilaterally of any 10,000 of their weapons to get the ball rolling. I added that President Bush would almost be forced to follow suit because the American public would not want to afford either the expense or the risks of retaining more of these weapons than we needed.

Akhromeyev was cool to the idea and said the United States would have to go first. I pointed out that I was a lonely voice on this issue in the United States and was not in a position of authority. He was better placed to plant the seed. He dropped the issue and moved on.

About forty-five minutes later in our dialogue I came back to this idea. Akhromeyev was more contemplative and ended this second discussion by saying that maybe it was a good idea. Another forty-five minutes later, as the meeting was drawing to a close, he leaned over and asked, "Would you mind if I used your idea about 10,000 warheads with Gorbachev?" I parted feeling great warmth for the man and a ray of hope for the idea.

Ten months later Akhromeyev was dead. There had been an abortive coup attempt against Gorbachev. Whatever Akhromeyev's involvement, when it was all over he had taken his own life. If START II is implemented by 2007 as scheduled, each side will have reduced its strategic warheads by about 10,000 from what it had back then in 1990. I will always wonder whether, in the absence of the political machinations going on within the Kremlin, Akhromeyev might have been able to lead both countries to those reductions perhaps ten to fifteen years earlier.

IF PARITY WITH RUSSIA IS NOT ESSENTIAL, there are new opportunities for controlling nuclear weapons. We need not be limited by the painfully slow process of arms control agreements. We could take a leaf from one of the most successful efforts ever to limit nuclear arms. In September 1991 President Bush, using his authority as commander in chief, simply ordered almost all of our tactical nuclear weapons withdrawn from forward land bases and all naval ships, deactivated 450 ICBMs, and took our bomber fleet off alert. Soviet President Mikhail Gorbachev responded with similar actions nine days later.

A corresponding initiative could be taken today with strategic nuclear weapons. We could remove perhaps 1,000 warheads from operational strategic launchers and place them in *strategic escrow*,[1] that is, in designated storage areas some distance, say, 200 miles, from their launchers. We would invite the Russian Federation to place observers at each storage site. Their duties would be limited to counting the number of warheads going into storage, keeping track of whether any were removed, and conducting surprise inventories to ensure none had been clandestinely removed. They would also be allowed to check that other warheads had not been placed on the launch vehicles from which those in storage had been removed. These observers would have no authority to prevent our removing any or all warheads from any storage facility. They would, however, warn Moscow if we did. There would be no need to negotiate detailed rules for these steps of verification, as all that would be required would be straightforward counting of numbers of warheads going in and out. We could establish simple ground rules: The observers would have access to the storage sites at any time; they could inspect warheads any way they wanted, but from the exterior of the warhead casing only. Cheating by placing elaborately faked warheads in storage could be attempted, but there are technical devices that should be able to determine from inspection limited to the outside whether a real or fake warhead is inside. Since the warheads would not be opened, neither side need be concerned that the other would gain significant intelligence through this process.

The hope is that the Russians would follow our example, as in 1991. If they did not, we would still have more ready warheads than we could possibly need, and we could always return our 1,000 and remount them on launch vehicles.

If the Russians did follow our lead, it would open the door to a rapid series of initiatives and reciprocations by both parties. There would be no need for protracted negotiations while quibbling over details. There would be no need for parliamentary approvals, though both presidents would have to build support in their legislatures. Both would want to point out that because the warheads would all be intact neither would have fewer than the other at any time. Moreover, there would be no violation of the U.S. Senate's reservation on START II that the president not let an imbalance develop that "could endanger our society." At the same time, this would be a more meaningful step than the detargeting and dealerting procedures we and the Russians have instituted in recent years, as reconstitution would take days or weeks, not minutes or hours. Moreover, it would start a process.

In that process we would sequester a second increment of warheads, perhaps 2,000–3,000. If the Russians followed, the process could gain real momentum. From the 1998 levels of about 7,000 operationally ready strategic warheads, both we and the Russians could be down to a number like 1,000 well before START II's 3,500-warhead target for 2007.

Once this process of strategic escrow through initiatives and reciprocation was well established, the two sides could move in a number of directions to reduce readiness without destroying weapons:

- Observers could be positioned at all storage sites for reserve warheads. Reserve warheads could be stored at some distance from the weapons systems to which they could be mated; for example, reserve ICBM warheads could be moved to storage sites on a strategic bomber base rather than at an ICBM complex, thereby ensuring it would take some time to move and mate them to delivery vehicles.
- Observers could also be placed at the existing storage sites where tactical warheads are currently stored. The warheads could be shuffled around, however, so that each type of tactical warhead would be stored at some distance from its delivery system, for example, siting warheads for air-launched cruise missiles on an army base for artillery, rather than on an airfield where the delivery aircraft are located. The United States could move its aircraft-launched tactical nuclear warheads in Europe back to the United States.
- Components, such as guidance sets from the weapons or plutonium pits from the warheads, could be removed and placed at separate storage sites to further complicate and delay reassembly. This process could still be reversed.
- Warheads could be dismantled. For the time being we should delay this, as it would result in a residue of enriched uranium or plutonium. Until there is greater assurance of firm control over all elements of Russia's nuclear programs, it will be preferable to store entire warheads rather than such fissionable materials, which are more readily pilfered. In addition, Russian fissionable material is under the control of a civilian agency, Minatom. The Russian military, which has better security than Minatom, controls warheads.

The Russians and we would keep the START process going in parallel. Under it we would be destroying warheads down to agreed numbers as rapidly as dismantling facilities permitted. Progressively we would want to go from a total of 3,500 deployed warheads under START II, all the way down to about 200 fully ready. That would make the world safer by taking the two major arsenals below each other's point of non-recovery. It would leave more than enough capability for damage to be a strong deterrent. On the way to 200, however, we would have to bring in the other six nuclear powers whose arsenals range from about 500 warheads downward. This would mean a multinational treaty.

First, that treaty would provide the inspection mechanism to ensure no nuclear power was hiding warheads. Second, it would establish procedures under which all eight nuclear powers would ease their final 200 deployed warheads into escrow. Talk of going to low numbers of total weapons in escrow can arouse concern about vulnerability to surprise attack. Some people conjure up an image of all of our escrowed warheads being in one storage site and vulnerable to attack by only a few weapons that might be sequestered away by some opponent. There is no need to be so naive. As the number of remaining warheads goes down, the more our storage would be arranged so that each warhead would be in a separate, hardened location. That would mean that any disabling attack would take a lot of warheads and, hence, a lot of cheating. Beyond that, the last warheads we would place in escrow would come from the last SSBN. In short, we would keep a secure retaliatory capability at sea until we were very confident of the security of what was stored ashore. Nonetheless, the negotiations to get to a very low total number and all in escrow will be difficult. Once the escrow process is started, however, we could begin discussions and carry them on during the several years it would take to implement strategic escrow.

The endpoint of a program of strategic escrow, then, would be:

- All nuclear warheads in the world in internationally supervised storage at some distance from their launchers.
- A limit of not more than 200 warheads and accompanying launchers for each of eight nuclear powers.
- Observers to provide warning of any effort to mate warheads to launch vehicles.

There are three principal impediments to getting a process of strategic escrow off the ground: Whether either the United States or Russia would be willing to start it; whether the other would be willing to reciprocate; and whether there would be sufficient commitment on both sides to find the resources to carry it out.

Just a few years ago, the fixation in the United States with numerical parity and our ingrained distrust of Russia would have made the unilateral initiatives of a strategic escrow program politically unfeasible for the United States. Today, the Cold War is behind us and we have the opportunity to play from our strength to lessen the nuclear threat. The issue is whether political leaders in both the administration and U.S. Congress will risk antagonizing segments of the population that still fear even a weakened Russia.

In Russia, there would be strong opposition to reducing nuclear strength. Moreover, the parlous state of Russia's conventional forces—witness their poor performance in Chechnya—has resulted in a prevalent argument for relying more on nuclear forces. The Russians cannot do that, however. They simply will not have enough nuclear weapons. A Russian deputy prime minister, Yuri Maslyukov, has said quite explicitly that Russia's nuclear weapons are fast becoming obsolete. He forecast that because of financial limitations "the most we can hope for is several hundred nuclear charges in 2007–2010."[2] Evidence that the Russians do not have the resources to replace nuclear delivery missiles as they wear out is that they produced and delivered only two new ICBMs in 1997. Moreover, as my earlier conversation with Marshal Akhromeyev evidenced, informed Russians understand that lower numbers are desirable. The larger the handwriting on the wall becomes, the more seriously Russians will have to take a proposal like strategic escrow. They will badly need some way to avoid letting a huge discrepancy between the size of their arsenal and ours become too obvious. And because the Russian president has greater room for maneuver in areas such as this than does the U.S. president, it is just as conceivable that Russia could make the initial move into strategic escrow. Our strengths permit us either to follow their lead or to initiate escrow; Russian weaknesses will force them either to lead or to follow.

The most serious constraint on strategic escrow would be a lack of storage space. The number and location of available storage facilities for nuclear weapons in the United States are kept secret. It is difficult to believe, however, that in a system as large as ours has been, there would not be space immediately available for several thousand extra warheads to get

Phase 1 started. We would then need only 3,000–5,000 additional storage spaces, and we are already dismantling warheads at a rate of about 1,500 per year, which opens up storage. We can also shift storage around, as suggested above, by placing one kind of warhead in storage facilities for another so as to separate warheads from their launch vehicles. I doubt it would be necessary, but we might have to rehabilitate or expand old storage sites or even build new ones. The construction would be simple: concrete bunkers suitably spaced, with some maintenance facilities in which to conduct checks on safety and operational readiness. In fact, much of the needed storage space need not be that elaborate. Maintenance and test facilities are required only if there is some possibility of putting the weapons back on line some day. That will not be the case with many warheads that go into escrow. Today, for instance, we have agreed with the Russians to go down to 3,500 deployed warheads. There is no necessity for ensuring the future usefulness of warheads in escrow above that number. They are already on the block to be destroyed. There is simply inadequate capacity to dismantle them immediately. We could also likely get agreement with the Russians that there is no need to maintain the future viability of most tactical nuclear weapons—witness how quickly and easily we both withdrew them in 1991 from where they were most likely to be used. We could also try to get agreement that reserve warheads make little sense and classify them as expendable.

From inquiries I made in Moscow during 1998, I believe Russia would have a larger problem with storage. Estimates I was given ranged from "absolutely no available storage space" to "a modest amount." Clearly the Russians, having had to reabsorb all the warheads they had placed in Kazakhstan, Belarus, and Ukraine, have reason to be crowded. There are a number of potential solutions:

- The United States can help Russia build storage facilities that meet the minimal standard of safety, using funding from the Cooperative Threat Reduction (CTR) Program established by the U.S. Congress.
- The United States and Russia can work cooperatively to accelerate construction, already in progress under the CTR Program, for fissile material being removed from Russian warheads. Warheads, neutered by having their fissile components removed, could be

  removed from normal storage space to make room for warheads
  under escrow.
- Using excess ICBM silos for storage, rather than dismantling
  them completely.
- We could temporarily reduce the size of the storage requirement
  by removing and storing plutonium pits rather than complete
  warheads. That, however, would be less desirable than storing
  warheads, as it would be less of an impediment to rebuilding and
  less of a symbol of the downgrading of nuclear weapons.

There will certainly be problems of storage in both countries, but not
insuperable ones. The real issue comes down to political will. The technical issues can be overcome, and with ingenuity there need not be any
great delay.

A form of strategic escrow could and should be applied to chemical
and biological weapons also by placing international observers at sites
where chemical agents or weapons are awaiting destruction. The observers would have authority only to report if weapons were being removed. Because of the number of nations involved, this could only be
done by amending the Chemical and Biological Warfare Conventions.

6

NO FIRST-USE

IN SEPTEMBER 1975, I was appointed commander in chief of NATO's southern flank, based in Naples, Italy. The responsibilities of this command included the defense of Italy, Greece, and Turkey from invasion by land. Being a naval officer, I needed to learn a good deal about the tactics of ground warfare. One concern that intrigued me about land defenses was how we would stop an assault into northern Italy. An approach the Warsaw Pact could take would be to drive from Eastern Europe across Austria and south over the Brenner Pass through the Alps. I assumed we had a good chance of disrupting such a large-scale movement in the mountains, but I wanted to know just how. I decided to start by talking with Colonel John B. Keeley of the U.S. Army, a good friend who I knew to have an imaginative approach to such problems. Just before coming to the staff of the southern flank, John had commanded the 2nd Brigade of the U.S. Army's 3rd Armored Division. This brigade was positioned astride Fulda Gap, the principal invasion route from Eastern Europe into West Germany. Although the terrain at the gap was different from that at the Brenner Pass, I wanted to talk to John about defense of passes and gaps.

John described the tactics he and his superiors had envisioned for plugging the Fulda. He mentioned they included atomic demolition munitions (ADMs) to blow up a hillside and send debris cascading onto a key highway. With a wry smile, John said he had an interesting story about these munitions. During his tour in command, the brigade had been relocated from one position to another just a few miles away. That made it necessary for John to adapt his plans to the differences in terrain. He discovered there was no sensible way to employ ADMs in the new location. He sent his plan for defending his portion of the gap without use of ADMs up the chain of command. It quickly came back disapproved. His superiors said the ADMs simply had to be included. Argue as he might, John found there was no way he could turn in the ADMs or just hold them in reserve. He had to find the least worst way to incorporate them into his plan. That left him the dilemma of what he would actually do in the event of war. It was clear the purpose of these weapons was more for deterrence than for fighting.

That discussion prompted me to ask about the ADMs assigned to my command, and this brought me back to the Brenner Pass. It turned out our war plans employed ADMs to destroy concrete pylons about 150 feet high that underpinned the mountainous highway coming through the Brenner. The briefer showed me pictures of the road literally clinging to the mountainside with the support of many of these pylons. In the photos they stood out as narrow, stark-white streaks against the background of the gray mountainside and looked very vulnerable. I asked whether charges of conventional explosives could not readily topple them. A stunned silence followed. It was clear this had not been considered. The fact that we had nuclear weapons that would do the job more assuredly than any other option was enough. There were no calculations to compare not only the effectiveness of the two kinds of explosives but also their ancillary effects, like radioactive fallout, fires, and electromagnetic interference. Getting the road closed and making use of these weapons, not the total consequences, were what mattered.

I did not attempt to take these ADMs out of the war plans. It was not worth the probable arguments. I just assumed I would not use them if war came.

It would be out of character for the United States to initiate the use of nuclear weapons today despite our having done so on two occasions in 1945. Our adherence to the Chemical and Biological Warfare Conventions makes it clear we do not intend to use those types of weapons first, either. We still remain the only nation to have used nuclear weapons. President Harry Truman made that fateful decision, at the end of an era when we thought our existence as a society was at stake. The subsequent Cold War era was another in which we thought we were again at such risk. The post–Cold War era, however, cannot be so characterized. The prospect of our coming under another deadly threat is sufficiently distant that if we forsake the first-use of nuclear weapons, doing so will not jeopardize our security. This includes our pledge in 1952 to use nuclear weapons in aid of our European allies if they were being overwhelmed by a conventional assault. With the end of the Cold War, we have already put additional distance between ourselves and this nuclear guarantee by emphasizing that any use of nuclear weapons on behalf of allies would be a "last resort."[1]

The next step would be to renounce the pledge altogether, but this immediately becomes an emotionally charged issue. There are arguments, then, that Germany would thereby be driven to acquire its own nuclear weapons, that NATO's very fabric would be rent, and that the United States would be seen as an unreliable ally. In contrast there is sentiment in Germany today in favor of NATO's making a pledge of no first-use of nuclear weapons, and in Canada also.[2] It is also important to recognize that the U.S. 1952 pledge of a nuclear response is to a *conventional* attack, not to a nuclear one. There has always been a question as to whether we would honor this pledge. As noted earlier, Henry Kissinger cautioned the allies not to count on us. French President Charles de Gaulle felt the same way and said, "No one in the world, and in particular no one in America, can say whether or where or how or to what extent American nuclear weapons would be used to defend Europe."[3]

Today, there is not the slightest prospect of our being called upon to honor this commitment. The countries of the defunct Warsaw Pact, former Soviet allies, are now a buffer between Russia and Western Europe. The Soviet military, once perceived as almost invincible, has withered to the point of defeat in Afghanistan and Chechnya. Even if Russia resuscitates and grows belligerent again, there is no reason to believe conventional defenses could not deal with any conventional assault it might launch. Russia retained only 49 percent of the Soviet Union's population and 60 percent of its GDP, which has fallen dramatically since. The current NATO states will be well ahead economically for a very long time. If Russia does close the gap, NATO would only need to calibrate its conventional force levels to the size and shape of whatever conventional threat reemerges. Whether we and our allies choose to afford the appropriate level of con-

ventional forces is, of course, open to question. Continuing to rely on a nuclear threat, however, would make maintaining adequate conventional
forces less likely. Where the European allies, the Germans in particular, do
need a U.S. pledge of nuclear support is in the event of nuclear attack.
There is no thought of our walking away from that commitment, and I
suggest later in this chapter that we would do well to expand it.

This does not mean that our canceling the U.S. nuclear guarantee
against conventional attack would be accepted readily. Our European allies usually balk at any change to NATO they interpret as another step toward U.S. disengagement from Europe. During the summer of 1998,
when I discussed this issue with government officials in London, Bonn,
Paris, and Ankara, there was limited receptivity. In Paris a senior retired
French diplomat and I jousted on this for some time. He finally threw up
his hands: "Monsieur, you do not understand. This is not a military or political problem, it is a psychological one." Indeed, that it is, and it must be
treated as such. The psychology is that of a warm, familiar U.S. security
blanket the Europeans do not want to abandon just because it is no longer
needed. We will have to nurture them along, but the logic is too strong for
them to resist indefinitely, as indicated by the fact that the Germans and
Canadians have raised the issue.

If we do not maintain our nuclear pledge to current allies, we certainly
would not extend one to the three East European states have been
brought into NATO. They must surely desire a nuclear umbrella, but the
problems with our extending one would be significant. We have always
rationalized that in defending NATO our nuclear attacks could be limited
to targets in Eastern Europe, meaning any response would most likely be
on Western Europe, not the United States. As NATO expands eastward as
planned, it will find itself on the doorstep of Russia (assuming Russia re-
absorbs Belarus and Ukraine). Thus, any nuclear attack would have to be
aimed at the Russian homeland. Any retaliation, then, would most likely
fall against the United States. Exposing the United States to nuclear retaliation in order to defend Eastern Europe is more commitment than we
should, or will, undertake.

If we were to withdraw our nuclear guarantee in Europe, a strong case
could be made for doing the same in Asia. It could be argued, however,
that this would make China a greater threat to our allies in the region.
There is, though, a high probability we could defend South Korea, Taiwan,

and Japan from Chinese attacks with conventional forces. We have done it once in Korea; Taiwan and Japan are more readily defensible because they are islands. Conventional defenses would be preferable, since China has an intercontinental ballistic missile capability that exceeds our point of self-deterrence. The reality our friends and allies all around the world need to face is that for more than a half-century the tradition of no first-use has been firmly established. No nuclear power has found an objective of foreign policy worth the risk of nuclear retaliation. And even in circumstances where nuclear retaliation was unlikely, the use of a nuclear weapon has never been deemed appropriate. Wars were lost, major powers were humiliated, but the nuclear trigger was not pulled, for example, by the United States in Korea and Vietnam and by the Soviet Union in Afghanistan and Chechnya. Establishing a worldwide policy of no first-use would simply be acknowledging reality.

The strongest argument against a pledge of no first-use is that there are benefits from a posture of calculated ambiguity. The *implied* threat of nuclear attack might be just what it takes to deter some would-be aggressor. As already suggested in the context of deterring chemical and biological weapons attacks, no such aggressor could afford to assume we meant what we said if we pledged no first-use. At the same time, however, by reserving our right to first-use to protect our interests, we directly undermine our efforts to deny others nuclear weapons. There are, then, two differing perspectives on the doctrine of no first-use. One emphasizes deterring nuclear, chemical, biological, and even conventional attacks by maintaining ambiguity as to how we would respond. The other emphasizes consistency in our position against proliferation by unambiguously denying the utility of these weapons. We need to adopt the longer-range view of preventing proliferation, rather than the more questionable and immediate one of bluffing with nuclear threats. If we did, this would also be an important step in encouraging others in this direction.

We could then attempt to get Russia to agree to a bilateral statement renouncing first-use. Such a declaratory statement would not require extensive negotiation and ratification by the U.S. Senate, as with a treaty. Russia had such a pledge but in 1993 withdrew it out of concern for the declining capability of its conventional forces. Specifically, the Russians have China and various Muslim states on their borders in mind. In reality, Russia is self-deterred in both cases: with China because of the high probability of nuclear retaliation; with the Muslims because use of nuclear weapons would either be disproportionate or not useful in achieving their objectives (presumably a key reason Russia did not use them in Chechnya and Afghanistan).

China has always had a pledge of no first-use and, hopefully, could be brought into a three-way statement with Russia and the United States. That would place considerable pressure on Britain and France, even on Pakistan, India, and Israel. France and Britain would likely balk out of concern for lessening the role of the United States in NATO but could find themselves isolated if Germany, Canada, the United States, and perhaps one or two others favored no first-use. With India and Pakistan, there is a great deal of logic to agreeing to a pledge of no first-use. India wants to deter China from conventional attacks by threatening nuclear retaliation. Both sides know, however, that it would be suicidal for India to use nuclear weapons against China. And both India and Pakistan should want to keep their intense rivalry from going nuclear. Israel would certainly be reluctant to give away what it sees as a deterrent to an overwhelming Arab conventional attack. Israelis know, however, that their use of a nuclear weapon against any Arab state could coalesce the fractious Arabs and lead to Israel's ultimate defeat. Pledging not to use nuclear weapons first could encourage Israel to pay adequate attention to conventional defenses so as not to risk being pushed against a nuclear extremity.

A world in which all nuclear powers had pledged not to use these weapons first would be a big improvement over today, when every nation lives under some threat of nuclear devastation from these powers.

7

DEFENSES

On December 7, 1941, I was a freshman at Amherst College in Amherst, Massachusetts. During the late afternoon I was walking outside the dormitory when someone shouted out of a window, "Japan has attacked Pearl Harbor." Groups of us students spent the remainder of December 7th glued to the radio while discussing how going to war would affect our college programs. Little did I imagine it would reshape not just my college routine, but my entire life.

A few months later I made my first move into what became my career—trying to contribute to national security. I did it by volunteering for the Amherst College Fire Brigade. Until that point, the college had no fire department but relied on the two-engine firehouse in the city of Amherst, less than a half-mile from campus. Suddenly, the assistant dean discovered that the war had made Amherst College a strategic target. The college is located about fifteen miles almost due north of Westover, Massachusetts, site of what was then a sizable Army Air Corps base. The campus sits on a prominent hill dominated by a lovely chapel with a typical New England white steeple. The assistant dean's conclusion was that German bombers heading for Westover would use our chapel as a navigational landmark. More than that, lead bombers would drop incendiaries on the chapel so as to make it highly visible, day or night. The college needed an instant fire brigade to deal with this threat to the historic chapel and even to the entire campus. We also, of course, hoped that in extinguishing the fire we would make it difficult for the Germans to find Westover Air Base.

Somewhere the assistant dean acquired a respectable, used fire engine for this purpose. He then solicited students to operate it. On weekends we volunteer firemen would drive conspicuously around the campus in our fire engine, stopping for a training drill at some unsuspecting building that might be hazarded one day by the Germans. We learned to unroll the hoses in quick time and which way to point the nozzles. The only fire on the campus during my remaining time at Amherst was in a fraternity house amid a boisterous party one Saturday night. Unfortunately, many of our fire brigade were not fit for duty at that moment. The city's firemen came to the rescue of Delta Kappa Epsilon.

Somehow none of us asked the assistant dean too probingly whether the Luftwaffe had aircraft that could fly all the way from Germany to Amherst. Or, if they could, whether it was conceivable they could fly home again after destroying our chapel. We also didn't question whether the Germans, if they could find our little chapel after flying perhaps 5,500 miles, might find Westover Air Base on their own? My first contribution to national security may have been of questionable importance, but it was a start.

THERE HAVE BEEN MORE SERIOUS and egregious examples of overreaction to supposed threats to our national security than the Amherst College Fire Brigade. Our interment of Japanese Americans during World War II stands out as one. Today, some individuals say we are overreacting, others that we are underreacting, to the threat on our country of ballistic missile attacks. The one side believes we are asking for another Pearl Harbor if we do not move rapidly to counter this threat, which, supposedly, is clearly foreseeable. The other side believes that if we do move urgently toward such defenses we will rupture a treaty that, supposedly, is key to all further nuclear arms control agreements. Why are feelings so strong?

On the side of building defenses, Americans are understandably uncomfortable with being vulnerable to ballistic missile attacks with nuclear warheads, despite having been so for more than thirty years. Just the fact that this has gone on for so long aggravates the issue, since Americans tend to assume problems can be solved. Also, in warfare the offense seldom remains dominant over the defense as long as it has in nuclear strategy. A new offensive measure has almost always led rather quickly to a defensive countermeasure, which in turn has led to an offensive counter-countermeasure. With nuclear weapons, because our point of self-deterrence is so low, that pattern has been interrupted; that is, defenses are worth building only if they would be very close to perfect. However, the traditional pendulum of defense-offense-defense is so ingrained that we have assumed defenses would play a role in nuclear strategy. As far back as the 1950s, we began spending large sums to render our strategic forces less vulnerable to surprise attacks. We created the North American Air Defense System, the Ballistic Missile Early Warning System, and an airborne alert system. In 1972, even though it was clear that constructing a meaningful defense against ballistic missiles was well beyond both U.S. and Soviet capabilities, we negotiated the Anti-Ballistic Missile (ABM) Treaty. It restricts the defenses each side could build. We went on to build one of the two ABM systems each side was permitted. Then, in 1983, President Ronald Reagan originated the Strategic Defense Initiative (SDI). He was persuaded that new technologies would enable us to construct a virtual umbrella over the entire United States that would be impervious to ballistic missiles. After spending some $50 billion, we have scaled down this ambition.[1] Even those who are most hopeful now look for a nation-wide defense against only a very limited number of ballistic missiles. Still, the impulse to defend ourselves remains strong and has even been strengthened by the growing possibility of chemical or biological warheads, as well as nuclear, being employed on ballistic missiles.

The other side calls national ballistic defense a Maginot Line and strongly opposes it on the thesis that should we build defenses the Russians would retain more offensive nuclear forces to compensate. This, in turn, would rupture the nuclear arms control treaty process. For some time we have suspected this was not a realistic possibility, and, as noted earlier, the Russians have now confirmed that they could do nothing of the sort. Setting reality aside, a complex argument has been developed that we must, nonetheless, preserve the ABM Treaty.

The premises of this argument are that the United States will build perfect defenses against ballistic missile attacks; be capable of conducting a preemptive attack that will destroy nearly 100 percent of Russia's offensive forces; and feel comfortable that its defenses could deflect any residual Russian forces that might survive to retaliate. The conclusion, then, is that Russia has reason to retain larger offensive nuclear forces than it might otherwise in order to make it more difficult for us to pull off such a scheme. Every one of these premises is erroneous.

To begin with, the technical challenges of building perfect ballistic missile defenses are not only formidable; no matter what the technicians invent, in war there is, as Clausewitz termed it, "friction" and "the fog of war": People make mistakes; equipment does not perform up to standards; the enemy responds in unexpected ways; uncontrollable forces like the weather interfere. As a result, there will never be a foolproof defense against ballistic missiles. Nor will any preemptive strike on our part be close to perfect. For instance, U.S. ICBMs will not be fully reliable; indeed, some will not even get off the ground, some will not reach Russia, some will get there but not come close enough to their target, and some will arrive at the target but not detonate. On top of operational shortcomings, intelligence will never be entirely accurate. Very likely we will not be able to locate some Russian forces, most particularly their land-mobile ICBMs and large stockpile of tactical nuclear weapons. Besides that, a U.S. preemptive strike on all of Russia's nuclear forces is out of the question on moral grounds. It would require thousands of large nuclear warheads and would very likely end Russia as a society. The unavoidable radioactivity could contaminate many other societies, including our own. No U.S. president would take such a risk, especially when there is no reason to attack Russia's nuclear forces. Russia can only challenge us today with nuclear weapons. It would be foolish to force them onto that turf.

Thus, we will never feel comfortable in initiating nuclear war because neither our defenses nor our offense can give assurance our point of self-deterrence will not always be exceeded. For instance, if Russia's nuclear forces were at a level of 3,000 warheads and we assume—unrealistically but to present an extreme case—that our preemptive attack is 90 percent successful against immobile weapons and 50 percent against mobile ones, that we have ballistic missile defenses that are 70 percent effective, and that only 10 percent of Russia's weapons fail due to friction, then the number of Russian warheads impacting on the United States would be a clearly unacceptable 539. At even less realistic figures of 90 percent effective ballistic missile defenses and 50 percent Russian failures due to friction, the United States would still receive 233 detonations. If in the future the United States and Russia each reduce arsenals to 1,000 warheads, under the original assumptions seventy-eight warheads would survive and penetrate to the United States. With only 250 warheads each, twenty would still impact on the United States.* It is difficult to imagine that a president could justify initiating a nuclear war that resulted in the loss of even one American city, let alone twenty.

Concern that the Russians would retain more offensive forces to counter our defenses, then, is not warranted. We should not, then, let a fallacious theorem dictate our position on national ballistic missile defense. Instead, we should decide how rapidly to proceed based on a continuing assessment of the threats we are likely to face, the effectiveness of defenses we could build, the cost of those defenses, and any political ramifications from building a national defense.

Threats: The most publicized controversy over ballistic missile defenses centers on when additional nations may be able to threaten the United States with ballistic missiles. Currently only Russia and China have that ability (excepting Britain and France). The question is whether potentially hostile nations, such as Iraq and Iran, will develop ballistic missiles that could reach the United States. In 1995 the Director of Central Intelligence estimated it would be ten to fifteen years before nations like these would be able to produce missiles capable of reaching the U.S. mainland (the estimate found that North Korea would most likely develop missiles capable of reaching the western parts of Alaska and Hawaii within this time frame). A skeptical Congress mandated a special commission to evaluate that conclusion. It reported in July 1998 that a few countries like Iran and North Korea could have an intercontinental ballistic missile capability within five years, and Iraq in ten years, and that we might not have much warning about these developments. The study group did not predict this would actually happen. Rather it made the case that it could be done. This dispute over whether this new threat is five, ten, or fifteen years away is not truly consequential. Ballistic missiles are going to proliferate. The issue is this: When it happens, will it be a serious threat to the United States?

The answer is no, because rogue states that acquire ICBMs will hesitate to employ them against the United States. They know the risk of severe retaliation would be very high. Even while their first missile was en route to the United States we would be backtracking its trajectory and identifying

---

*The calculations behind these numbers are given in Appendix C.

its exact point of launch. And operational ICBMs are too conspicuous for us not to know who has them. Although no one can give assurance as to how a president would react to a ballistic missile attack from a rogue state, a rogue leader would be naive to assume his country might not be devastated in retaliation, even that he might not survive.* This is not to say that rogue states will not seek to acquire ballistic missiles with nuclear, chemical, and biological warheads. They will want them in the hope of deterring the United States from intervening in their affairs. Would we, for instance, have been as willing to go to the rescue of Kuwait in 1990 had Iraq possessed nuclear weapons? Rogue states might know full well that they would never fire a ballistic missile at the United States but still want the capability to threaten to do so. Because deliberate attacks on the United States with ballistic missiles could be deemed too risky by any aggressor, we need to concentrate on how weapons of mass destruction might be delivered more anonymously by hostile powers. One of these would be by a cruise missile attack on a U.S. city from a merchant ship off our coast. Another would be by smuggling weapons of mass destruction into the United States. This could be in a ship of almost any size coming into one of our ports; an aircraft, ranging from a national airliner to a private aircraft, arriving at an airport; or just a truck coming across the Mexican or Canadian border. Biological and chemical weapons manufactured surreptitiously in the United States are also a significant threat.

The prospect of an aggressor employing one of these clandestine approaches in preference to ballistic missiles is reinforced by the fact that from the point of view of most rogue states biological and chemical weapons are better suited to such unconventional delivery than missiles. This is because the delivery of chemical and biological agents by aerosol spray is much more effective than with an explosive missile. Another possibility for attacks is the secret placement of chemical and biological agents, as with the Aum Shinrikyo in the Tokyo subway system. This is an even more easily engineered option, even though such attacks would likely not be as lethal as those using other methods of delivery. In addition, rogue states and terrorists will most likely find biological and chem-

*It is sometimes argued that ballistic missile defenses are useful in deterring other nations from acquiring small nuclear arsenals that likely could not penetrate them. In fact the threat of overwhelming retaliation by us is an adequate deterrent.

ical weapons easier to obtain than nuclear. The technological barriers for manufacturing nuclear weapons are much higher and more unique than those of producing toxic agents or of fermenting biological agents through commercially available dual-use equipment.

On balance, with the end of the Cold War, the threat of deliberate ballistic missile attacks on the United States from Russia, or even China, has declined markedly, and the new threat of attacks with ballistic missiles by rogue states is not high. That leaves us, though, with the danger that has always been there: the possible launch of one or a few missiles by Russia or China by accident or miscalculation or without authorization. The economic and political chaos in Russia today has increased the probability of this threat. This prospect of accident, then, is what defines the effectiveness we will require in a defensive system. It should be capable of instant response without warning and have a reasonably high probability of defeating a small attack. It need not aspire to the SDI goal of an impregnable shield against a massive attack.

Effectiveness: In estimating whether new defensive systems we might want to develop will measure up to such a standard, we are faced with the age-old problem that expectations for new weapons are always overly optimistic. There are predictions today that new techniques will enable U.S. defenses against limited attacks by ballistic missiles to be 90 percent effective. Having heard similar forecasts for SDI, we ought to judge this against the recent, and only, actual evidence of our defensive capabilities. During the Gulf War, we employed Patriot missiles to defend against Russian SCUD ballistic missiles fired by Iraq against Israel and against U.S. forces in Saudi Arabia. Estimates of the results range from very modest success to the failure to destroy even a single warhead.[2] This is despite the fact that Patriot had enjoyed a good record during testing.* Shooting down ballistic missiles is a formidable technical challenge. To expect 90 percent success is being very optimistic, just from the technical aspect. Beyond that, the interplay of defense and offense comes into action. As the capability of defenses mount, an attacker could complicate and confuse those defenses,

---

*It must be acknowledged that Patriot was designed for defending against aircraft and upgraded to deal with ballistic missiles. Still, it was the only antiballistic missile defense system we had available.

requiring even more sophistication in the defenses. Estimating even 60–70 percent success against ballistic missile attacks within a decade would be extremely risky until we have solid evidence from a program of testing. This is not to say that defensive technologies will not improve, just that a cautious skepticism is warranted after many years of meager results.

Costs: We should be wary of unrealistically low estimates of the costs of defenses. With almost all new weapons systems, there are cost overruns. The fact that we have spent more than $50 billion on SDI shows how easy it is for vast sums to disappear with very limited results. We should not make a decision to procure a new system if we are not willing to pay at least half again the estimated price.

Political Ramifications: Although the Russian position that they would retain more nuclear systems if we should build strategic defenses does not make sense and is not viable, that does not mean the Russians will not cause problems should we break the ABM Treaty. We should not, then, needlessly aggravate them by rupturing that treaty before absolutely necessary. We should even look for ways to assuage concerns in Russia that our building defenses is part of an attempt to gain additional advantage over them through manipulating the nuclear balance. We could pledge not to introduce nuclear weapons into Poland, the Czech Republic, and Hungary now that they have joined the North Altantic Treaty Organization (NATO). (This might require extending that pledge to all of NATO, which would be a good move anyway.) Another step would be to discontinue our long-standing practice of patrolling the Barents Sea with U.S. attack submarines to keep track of Russian submarine activities. The impunity with which we operate in their backyard is galling to them. Today Russian submarine operations are so limited that this surveillance cannot be very interesting or important. Satellite surveillance of their ports will alert us if they start sending serious numbers of submarines to sea again. We could also withdraw our SSBN patrols out of range of Russia. We have no conceivable need to have them ready for immediate response. Withdrawal could not be verified in entirety without a very detailed treaty, but we could occasionally expose an SSBN to Russian satellite observation to show that it was out of range. And we could renew the offer President Reagan made in connection with SDI to share our research on defenses.

We could invite capable Russian scientists to work alongside our scientists. If, from this, the Russians understood that the best we could hope for was to defeat small attacks, as would very likely be the case, they would see that the strategic balance could not be upset by proceeding with the best defenses we might build.

China would also be sensitive to our building defenses against ballistic missiles. They have already objected to the possibility of our giving ballistic missile defense technologies to Taiwan and Japan. Presumably they are concerned that Japan and Taiwan might be more aggressive toward China if they did not have to take into account the Chinese nuclear capability. The Chinese concern, however, does not have merit. China's roughly 500 nuclear warheads could easily overwhelm any Japanese or Taiwanese defenses. In addition, those countries pose no military threat to China. The unspoken concern behind the Chinese protest is that China's threat to the United States with its ICBMs would be weakened if we possessed even modest defenses. The Chinese did threaten us in 1996 during a crisis between them and the Taiwanese when they pointedly and publicly reminded us that their ICBMs could reach Los Angeles. The obvious implication was that we should be wary of intervening on the side of Taiwan. It will, then, be difficult to assuage the Chinese, but Chinese security concerns could be defused somewhat by pointing out to them that the kind of defenses Japan and Taiwan require are closer to theater defenses than to national ones and that we have such an urgent need for these that we must develop them. We have only to look back to the Gulf War of 1991 to see that U.S. forces overseas, as well as allies like Japan and Taiwan, face a serious threat from shorter-range ballistic missiles. Twenty-eight U.S. military personnel were killed and ninety-eight wounded in their barracks in Saudi Arabia by one Iraqi SCUD ballistic missile.[3] Israel suffered some forty-one SCUD attacks with the loss of two people to direct hits and a number of others to indirect effects. Accordingly, we are today quite actively developing tactical and theater ballistic missile defense systems that will inevitably encroach on those provisions of the ABM Treaty designed to deny national defenses.

In our review of the four criteria enumerated above for whether to build a national ballistic missile defense, then, political ramifications should not deter us from proceeding with them; rather it is estimates of costs and effectiveness that will need to be balanced against our perception of threats. Those threats could be from the Russians making mistakes or rogues being irrational or terrorists hoping to remain anonymous through some esoteric technique. Which of those threats is the most serious is not of particular importance, because regardless of whether the prospects are for hundreds or tens of thousands of fatalities, Americans do not want to live under the shadow of actual nuclear, biological, or chemical attacks with ballistic missiles. Therefore, investing in defenses will always have an appeal.

Even more, two huge uncertainties are propelling us toward defenses. One is an abiding concern that somehow the Cold War will be revived; the other is where uncertainty as to new military technologies will take warfare. In my view, the impetus behind ballistic missile defenses today is an instinctive concern that developments in political or military arenas could threaten our national security. Ballistic missile defense is somehow seen as a hedge against both. In January 1999 President Bill Clinton acceded to these sentiments by suggesting the appropriation of more than $6 billion for the procurement of components of a national defense system, not just for research, which is what he had supported previously. He left open the decision as to when to commence construction. That leaves us with the issue of whether we will deploy a system before we have one with a meaningful capability, as we did during the 1970s. That will have to be determined by balancing our sense of urgency as to the threat with our sense of realism as to what capability is available.

Part of that calculation should be a comparison with investments we are making in defending against other methods of attack with weapons of mass destruction. We would be ill-advised to defend only against ballistic missiles. As mentioned earlier, cruise missiles launched from off our coasts are one alternative. Preventing such attacks by identifying and intercepting the ships or aircraft carrying the weapons of mass destruction would be an immense task, even if we had excellent intelligence. The Department of Defense states that it is working on the alternative of shooting down cruise missiles. That is akin to defenses against attacks by aircraft. Throughout the Cold War, we were conspicuously unable to construct an effective nationwide air defense system. Perhaps new technologies will make that possible in the future, but it is more likely that we will be limited to point defenses against very important targets, not national coverage.

The other, more surreptitious way of delivering weapons of mass destruction on the United States is through smuggling. Just being able to conduct surveillance of coastal areas and borders would require immense resources in the absence of exceptional intelligence. Any system of thorough inspection at airports, harbors, and borders could involve inordinate delays in routine travel. It would also require the development of new techniques for detecting radioactivity and biological and chemical agents. The American public would likely tolerate the required intrusiveness and inconvenience only if the reasons to do so were obvious, such as having experienced a prior nuclear, chemical, or biological incident. Still, we cannot wait until a crisis is upon us to make plans, train people, and develop the equipment needed should we find it necessary to tighten border controls. We must look at it as a military contingency plan. For instance, should we learn through intelligence sources that someone was going to attempt to smuggle a weapon of mass destruction across the Mexican border in a truck, we should be instantly ready to deploy the personnel and sensors to detect the weapons, as well as law enforcement officials to deter and interdict the smugglers. A host of U.S. agencies, including FEMA, the Federal Bureau of Investigation (FBI), the Department of Defense, and the Department of Energy, are reportedly working in this direction. We need to ensure that this work does not fall prey to institutional infighting.

Defenses against ballistic missiles, cruise missiles, and smuggling fall into the category of active military defenses. They are intended to prevent the arrival of any type of weapon of mass destruction on U.S. soil. We must also consider the category of passive civil defenses intended to help in weathering an attack and recovering from it. We attempted this with respect to nuclear attacks during the 1960s with a program of nationwide civil defense. Children were taught to dive under their desks at the sound of warning sirens; homeowners were urged to build bomb shelters and stock them with food and water; and plans to evacuate cities were developed and some drills attempted. The program, however, did not garner public support. It was both too expensive and inconvenient and was not persuasively useful anyway. Who could imagine the chaos of attempting to evacuate New York City in a few hours? What percentage of Americans would actually build bomb shelters? How long could we expect people to stay in them? And what would it be like to emerge from a shelter into a city that was devastated and radioactive? In time, we decided the threat of massive nuclear war was not that great. Subsequent efforts to regenerate interest in civil defense have failed. The growing problem of biological and chemical weapons has now reopened this issue of the viability of large-scale civil defenses as a means to counter or deter unconventional attacks on U.S. citizens. Although this debate will certainly generate criticisms similar to those of the nuclear civil defense program of the 1960s, the challenge of how to engage and motivate the public has been afforded a test case with the Israelis. In response to the threat during the Gulf War of an unconventional attack on its citizens with chemical or biological weapons from Iraq, the Israeli government developed a far-reaching program of public education and civil defense. Although the strategic environment is different in the United States, the Israeli model does provide an example of some of the possibilities for civil defense and preparedness. For instance, it demonstrated that it can be difficult to implement a preattack and postattack civil defense, even in a highly structured, educated society facing an eminent threat of chemical and biological attack. Yet it also shows that preattack preventive measures could make more of a difference than with nuclear attacks and that rapid postattack response and consequence management methods could save many lives and prevent further contamination.

The first line of such a preattack defense is inoculation. Inoculating 265 million Americans would be close to impossible. For instance, for just one biological agent, anthrax, six shots are required per person. About the only subset of people to be considered is the military. The U.S. military is already inoculating military personnel. Even this effort may turn out to be overreaching. An additional subset of people that should receive medical prophylaxis is medical personnel, especially those in emergency services. If those who rescue and treat victims of biological and chemical attacks become victims in the process, it can severely compound the problem, both through further contamination and reduced human resources to treat victims. Another segment of the population that could be a candidate for inoculation arises from the fact that a biological or chemical attack is likely to be limited to a few areas, not nationwide. In this regard, certain high-threat populations could be selected for inoculation, although even that would be a daunting task and a public relations challenge. The question of administering vaccines and antidotes to large portions of the population opens the possibility of stockpiling treatment supplies at central locations across the United States. In the event of an attack or threat of an attack, medical items could be flown quickly to the area in question. The effectiveness of this initiative is complicated by the fact that vaccines administered after exposure are considerably less effective—sometimes not at all, depending on the agent and the time lapse between initial exposure and administration of the dosage. A second impediment is knowing which vaccine or defensive injection to administer. It is impossible today to immunize against every possible agent, because an attacker's choices range from a few agents to almost an infinite number, depending on whether there is access to sophisticated laboratories. Only with very good intelligence, excellent deduction, and luck would we be likely to select the right vaccines. A third, more frightening possibility is that a sophisticated enemy could produce or acquire an agent against which known vaccines are ineffective by twisting advancements in molecular biology to malevolent ends. Such an attacker would either have to be a country with very advanced biological or chemical capabilities or be abetted by one. On the other side, it is possible that advances in the field of genetic engineering, including work on genomes, our basic genetic constitution, will result in so many avenues of defense as to overwhelm these and other types of germ attacks.

Another preattack, preventive measure is to maintain stocks of protective clothing. As a practical matter, protective clothing is likely to be useful only to troops operating in an environment where biological or chemical attack is probable. However, having protective clothing immediately available would have a high payoff for emergency medical personnel and nonmilitary decontamination teams. If medical personnel wear the right protective equipment, the capabilities to deal with and treat victims of chemical and/or biological weapons exposure are significantly strengthened. However, as with vaccines, there are immense problems of deciding how much protective clothing to store, where to store it, and how to train and maintain the appropriate people to use it.

A final preattack measure is to prevent the manufacture or delivery of biological and/or chemical weapons inside the United States either by foreign agents or dissident U.S. nationals. This requires trying to locate and identify very small scale, improvised manufacturing operations, as large quantities of agents are not needed to do large damage. At the same time, the very elaborate precautions required for the manufacture of biological agents can provide telltale indicators, as can sickness and deaths caused by the failure of such precautions. There also can be distinctive indicators of attempts at surreptitious delivery of chemical and/or biological agents (e.g., aircraft and trucks equipped with aerosol spraying equipment positioned in unusual places). This is principally a law enforcement challenge and falls under the cognizance of the FBI. The federal criminal statute regarding the possession of biological agents, however, needs to be improved. It is argued that strengthening it too far could inhibit legitimate research and intrude into the private activities of individuals, but we need to find an intermediate ground. We must also find ways to tap some 17,000 local, state, and federal law enforcement agencies, vast public health networks, even commercial companies that handle precursor chemicals and biological feedstocks. If these efforts are to be effective, some intrusion into the privacy of individuals and corporations will be necessary.

A second type of civil defense entails preparations for postattack treatment of victims. Most effects of biological and chemical agents can be treated after an attack, some only if done almost immediately after exposure. The key problem is to identify quickly that there has been an attack and then the precise agent used. Chemical agents can take hours to have a perceptible effect; it may take several days for the symptoms of a biological agent to appear. Even then, medical personnel need to diagnose the problem correctly, including correlating many victims showing similar symptoms. They need to be able to quickly recognize that they have encountered deliberate biological warfare, not a natural epidemic. In order to meet these challenges, a high-volume public health communication network with access to real-time information and diagnosis/treatment recommendations will be essential. This will take considerable and continual training of emergency response and medical treatment personnel. It will also require more research on equipment and techniques for identifying chemical and biological agents. Some exist today, but in the case of biological agents most measures take too long and are not able to detect a wide enough range of agent profiles. As with vaccines, being ready to treat even segments of 265 million people raises problems of sufficient stockpiling to make a difference; again, the attacker can attempt to use agents that are resistant to antibiotics.

As great as the obstacles may be, the imperative of self-defense is too strong to overlook. The very fact that we make an effort could discourage would-be aggressors who may overestimate the effectiveness of what we are doing. Even more, the interplay of activities in all three areas can have a cumulative impact greater than the sum of the individual efforts. For example, after going through inoculation, troops will very likely take defensive training drills more seriously; if an attacker modified the agent employed because a particular vaccine had been administered, the substituted agent might not be as lethal. In war, defense can be difficult, but it is not likely to be impossible. The issue, then, is how much effort to put into civil defenses and how to maximize the return.

In judging how large the investment should be for domestic preparedness and military defense in reaction to the chemical and biological threat, we should recognize that covert attacks are considerably more likely than ballistic missile attacks. This makes a prima facie case that we should be spending more on those defenses than on ballistic missile defense. It is almost impossible to calculate just how much is actually being spent against covert attacks because of the number of agencies involved. If, though, it were at all comparable to the $3–5 billion per year for ballistic missile defense, we would be more aware of how it was being spent.

Much of today's activity is stimulated by a 1996 act of Congress sponsored by U.S. Senators Sam Nunn, Richard Lugar, and Pete Domenici. It provided money for training first responders, established rapid response teams, and exercises to test responses. The program's focus is on 120 cities with populations more than 144,000 and containing 22 percent of the total U.S. population. Much training has been accomplished, but it has revealed that interagency coordination is lacking. Training courses overlap, federal funds pay for some equipment but not for maintenance, and direction to local authorities in any given area is likely to come from several federal agencies. Overlapping responsibility at the federal level is not unique to the issue of weapons of mass destruction. It is seldom that one agency of the federal government has sole responsibility or interest in some topic, but dealing with the effects of attacks by weapons of mass destruction is more complex than in almost any other issue. The agencies with overlapping authority and responsibility reach from the president's Cabinet and National Security Council (NSC) through some forty federal agencies, bureaus, and offices. There are seven federal agencies alone that maintain Emergency Support Teams. Moreover, this myriad of federal organizations must somehow coordinate with the numerous police and public health organizations within each of the fifty states and with fire, paramedic, and health units in each of countless local jurisdictions. Bureaucratic imperatives make it nearly impossible to place any one agency firmly in charge of such a wide, diverse set of organizations.

The way out of this morass of organizations and lack of central leadership is strong presidential direction, abetted by congressional actions. The first step should be to raise public consciousness about biological and chemical warfare without creating a sense of panic. This means acknowledging that the threats of biological and chemical warfare are indeed serious but that high fatalities are unlikely and that there are antidotes. Public awareness itself is a key element in defensive preparations.

Presidential leadership is also required in structuring the government to deal with issues more coherently. Despite bureaucratic resistance, one or more organizations must be charged with coordinating the actions for each type of defense. From my experience and observation, it is not enough simply to designate some individual on the staff of the National Security Council as coordinator of preparations for chemical and biological warfare, as has been done. Such an individual needs a backing organization that has independent sources of information and expertise, as well as the ability to direct actions. It also would not be adequate to create some "center" for dealing with chemical and biological warfare. Centers are useful for coordinating the flow of information—but not for taking action.

We need, then, to review the candidates for coordinating agencies. At the upper level, ballistic missile defense, there is no question the lead agency must continue to be the Department of Defense. At the next tier, defense against cruise missile attack, the Department of Defense clearly has the principal role to play. When it comes to controlling smuggling at borders and ports, the organizations involved multiply sharply and include the Departments of Defense, Justice, Commerce, Health and Human Services, and State, the Secret Service, the Immigration and Naturalization Service, the Customs Service, the CIA, the U.S. Marshal Service, the Coast Guard, the National Guard, the Bureau of Alcohol Tobacco and Firearms, the FBI, and state police. Numerous different skills from these organizations are needed to arrest smuggling, but the military skills of detecting, tracking, and neutralizing weapons coming at our country remain dominant. Defense is wary of becoming involved in law enforcement, but being in charge of antismuggling operations for chemical and biological weapons would not be like having Defense engage in fighting drugs and crime. Defending against ballistic and cruise missiles and mounting antismuggling operations, then, could easily be grouped together with responsibility for coordination assigned to the Department of Defense.

Plans for preattack preventive measures and postattack treatment involve quite different skills, primarily the responsibility for coordinating an enormous number of organizations, reaching from federal authorities down to local public health authorities. The coordinating organization must be located within the federal government, though, because funding for state and local activities must come from federal sources, as there is no hope that the thousands of state and local jurisdictions involved will find the funds to meet nationally prescribed standards. In dispensing funds, the federal agency responsible for coordination could encourage the needed standards of uniformity. Defense has the greatest capacity and best organizational skills to do this but would not be a good candidate, because preattack prevention and postattack treatment activities would compete with too many other department programs considered more important. Passive civil defenses would be submerged too far even if placed in a major department other than Defense. The FBI is a candidate, but it is not accustomed to coordinating multiagency operations. Besides, there is an inherent conflict between law enforcement and national security, with the one emphasizing obtaining convictions and the other preserving security.

The Federal Emergency Management Agency has the advantage, that coordinating the diverse activities of the aforementioned organizations would be closer to its current function (emergency planning and disaster relief). Moreover, this basic function already involves FEMA in most of the planned activities and programs related to civilian defense against chemical and biological weapons. FEMA, of course, lacks the stature of being a Cabinet department. It does, however, report directly to the president: If defense against biological and chemical warfare is a high priority on the president's agenda, FEMA's influence will grow.

The overall concept boils down to this: The Department of Defense and FEMA would bring together in two budget items all federal government activities, active and passive, to limit and control attacks with weapons of mass destruction. Defense and FEMA would do this by screening the requests of the various departments and agencies and placing them in priority. When the president approved these two budget plans for submission to Congress, he or she would be able to see the priority accorded each element. Either Defense or FEMA would testify before Congress alongside representatives of the organization that would spend the money. Once the money was appropriated by Congress, Defense and FEMA would dispense, withhold, or reallocate it. This partial budget control would give Defense and FEMA some leverage over federal departments and agencies, even over the state and local authorities involved. There would thus be an inducement to departments and agencies to think up new strategies for dealing with the problems because, if they could persuade the coordinating agency to place their programs in the budget item, they would get more money.

This is a way to manage the bureaucratic complexity of dealing with a problem that cuts across so many organizations. There certainly are other options. What we want to achieve is a solution that results as much as possible in a unitary direction of efforts while preserving the unique abilities and outlooks of the disparate organizations. One key to assessing the organizational arrangement would be periodic drills. Drills are particularly important, because they inevitably involve the public. If they are unrealistic, the public will kill them, as it did nuclear civil defense. The government will then have to reconsider its approach.

We, of course, will not limit ourselves to the largely domestic actions proposed in this chapter. Neither will we focus entirely on defenses. We will take the offense, preventing rogue nations and terrorists from even acquiring weapons of mass destruction and from employing them if they have acquired them. The steps needed to do that involve export controls, intelligence sharing, and international disapprobation. They require more than an effort by the United States, more even than by the United States and Russia together. The needed international effort is the subject of Chapter 8.

8

GLOBAL MANAGEMENT

IN MARCH 1977, JUST A WEEK after becoming Director of Central Intelligence, I attended my first meeting of the National Security Council in the Cabinet Room of the White House. The topic was forthcoming nuclear arms negotiations with the Soviet Union. The outgoing president, Gerald Ford, had left recently inaugurated President Jimmy Carter a nearly completed agreement, which we had been negotiating with the Soviet Union since November 1972. President Carter opened this meeting by saying he thought we could make much larger reductions than those in the draft agreement. To my amazement, he then briefed us on what he intended to propose to the Soviets. Even though he had been in office only two months, he knew as much about the topic as anyone in the room. Unfortunately, within a few weeks Soviet Secretary General Leonid Brezhnev had rejected President Carter's ambitious proposal out of hand. That sent us back to the drawing board and the process of negotiating terms with the Soviets, which would likely only split differences between the Ford and Carter proposals.

It was a painstaking effort first to get agreement from all of the parties involved on our side: the heads of the Arms Control and Disarmament Agency and the Departments of State, Defense, and Justice; myself; and, of course, the president. And to maneuver through the Byzantine bureaucracy in Moscow was not any easier. Sometimes U.S. Secretary of State Cyrus Vance would travel to Moscow; sometimes he would deal with the Soviet ambassador in Washington, Anatoly Dobrynin; other times he would leave it to a negotiating team permanently in Geneva. Whenever we thought we had some detail nailed down, a new wrinkle would develop somewhere in the Soviet system. After a year and a half we were making progress toward what was to be the Strategic Arms Limitation Treaty II (SALT II). Then, in December 1978, during discussions in Moscow, Cy Vance ran into several roadblocks with the Soviets that he could not overcome. He tossed them back to the National Security Council with his recommendations for adjustments we might make.

One of these was of key importance to my responsibility for ensuring that our intelligence mechanism could verify whatever terms were negotiated in the treaty. I believed we needed a provision prohibiting the Soviets from coding the telemetry signals from ICBMs that they test-fired. Telemetry is the means by which performance data generated inside a test missile are signaled back to the launchpad so the engineers can monitor the missile's performance. We could intercept telemetry signals and use the data to check on several provisions of the draft treaty (e.g., a missile's total carrying capacity). The Soviets had told Cy they would not include a prohibition against the coding of telemetry in the treaty; instead they would give us oral assurances. In the atmosphere of the Cold War it was difficult to accept such a promise, and this would have been particularly troubling to the U.S. Senate, which had to ratify any treaty we negotiated.

Cy was pressing for immediate instructions. We needed a meeting of the NSC, but President Carter was ill and in Plains, Georgia. Instead, there was a meeting that evening in Zbigniew Brzezinski's office. His office, with its high ceilings and eight-foot windows, which allowed one to look out onto the front lawn of the White House, normally seemed spacious and airy. But with every interested department and agency represented it was uncomfortably crowded, and most of us were juggling papers in our laps. We all hoped to avoid having to disturb the ill president to resolve any differences among us.

But there was this stumbling block of whether to insist on a provision against the coding of telemetry. I knew how much President Carter wanted this treaty. But I also knew that it might fail ratification if I could not give senators a firm assurance we could verify every provision quite precisely. Yet it was clear that all this anxiety over coding telemetry was a tempest in a teapot. So what if the Soviets cheated and added some warheads? They had more than 40,000 of them already. A few more would hardly be noticeable. However, it was not my responsibility to judge the political and military importance of Soviet cheating but to certify whether we could catch them reasonably quickly if they did. I believed we could do that only if there was no coding of telemetry.

I held to my position, which forced a phone call to the president. When Zbig got through to the Carter home in Plains, he was told the president had been sedated and was asleep. Zbig persisted, and as we waited he turned on a speaker on his desk so everyone could hear the president. When a groggy Jimmy Carter came on the line he must have expressed some considerable displeasure, because Zbig quickly turned off the speaker. We all listened to Zbig explain my position and the alternative of accepting oral assurances from the Soviets. The president decided to accept oral assurances. What really was at stake was persuading senators to ratify the treaty, and the president obviously understood our chances better than I did. It was clear nobody was concerned with the possibility of actual cheating.

Still, this issue of telemetry was consuming an inordinate amount of time of a number of the top leaders of our government; it was also threatening the impending treaty. Thus, the importance we had attached to nuclear parity was coming close to thwarting a historic effort at arms control. And given the large numbers of nuclear weapons on each side, that simply did not make any sense. For the next nine months, I worked diligently to persuade senators that we could check as closely as was necessary on the Soviets.

It looked as though reason would prevail and that telemetry would not be a roadblock to ratification. Then, on Christmas Day 1979 the Soviets invaded Afghanistan. SALT II came apart at the seams, and the president never even sent the draft treaty to the Senate for ratification.

THERE WILL ALMOST ALWAYS BE SOME ISSUE like telemetry that will intrude into an arms control negotiation and slow it down. Suspicions that the other side may find a way to gain advantage through cheating demand ironclad treaty terms. In the case of START II, negotiations began in 1987, but the best hope is that the treaty will be consummated in 2007, twenty years later. The BWC was negotiated more expeditiously between 1969 and 1972, but back then few nations had biological warfare programs and the potential for biological warfare was not seen as great. In contrast, because chemical weapons had been used in war and numerous countries had them, it took from 1969 to 1992 to negotiate the CWC.

After negotiating a treaty, it will take additional time to obtain parliamentary ratification. Here domestic politics intrudes; for instance, in the United States it is difficult to get the Senate to consider more than two arms control treaties in any year. Finally, it can take years to execute a treaty once ratified. Unfortunately, these delays will magnify as treaties work toward lower and lower numbers. If we nearly ruptured the SALT II process over a few warheads out of 40,000, we will want even more stringent terms when we get down to meaningful numbers. And when the numbers of permitted weapons approaches those of the other nuclear powers, they will have to be incorporated into the treaty process, complicating and slowing it.

What is equally disturbing about the current series of treaties on weapons of mass destruction is their limited effectiveness. As noted earlier, START II will take the United States down only to 10,000 warheads. Although that is progress relative to the 32,500 we had thirty years ago, it is not enough in the absolute to be meaningful reassurance. In the case of biological weapons, the BWC is little more than an exhortation because there is no provision for enforcement. Since 1994 the rate of progress on creating a process for effective enforcement has been glacial. As for the CWC, the original negotiation provided for verification, but countries have moved slowly in implementing it. Beyond that, at best it will be 2007 before the powers with large stocks of chemical weapons, Russia and the United States, are scheduled to have destroyed them; neither is likely to meet that deadline.

All this is not to say these agreements are not important. They set a norm for the world that weapons of mass destruction are to be phased out and never again developed. By focusing the concern of the world community on these areas of arms control, they make clandestine proliferation more difficult. If we had time to spare, there would be no problem. However, that is not the case. As we near the end of the millennium in a world convulsed by ideological, religious, and ethnic violence and deep economic inequalities, we cannot afford the luxury of such a dilatory pace. And if we look carefully, none of these agreements, even if carried out to the letter, will make significant differences for another five years. That pace is simply unrelated to the world in which we live. Russia and China are evolving in uncertain directions; states like Iran and Iraq are candidates for nuclear weapons within five years; and chemical and biological terrorism could certainly take place by then. Each of these classes of weapons of mass destruction—nuclear, biological, chemical— presents a slightly different challenge. We cannot abandon or neglect arms control treaties, but we need to find ways to accelerate the treaty process and to supplement it with immediate actions to reduce risks.

We already have the conventions that call for biological and chemical disarmament. There is increasing attention today to nuclear disarmament. Setting such a sweeping objective could energize people to move more rapidly. Nuclear disarmament, of course, is not new. Every U.S. president during the nuclear era has stated an explicit preference for zero nuclear weapons in the world. In signing the NPT the United States has pledged to work toward nuclear disarmament. And now more and more people of influence, such as former secretaries of defense, Nobel Peace Prize recipients, ambassadors, admirals, generals, and international figures from many other disciplines, have concluded that the objective of getting to zero nuclear weapons must drive our arms control efforts. This deserves careful consideration. It is clear to proponents and opponents alike that complete disarmament is not feasible in the foreseeable future because today no one knows how to take the last few steps from a few weapons to zero without risk that one of the nuclear powers would clandestinely retain some; neither is anyone confident that new nuclear powers might not arise after disarmament was achieved. Dealing confidently with these issues will require a regime for verification and control that would be light-years more comprehensive than anything we have today. It would need to include virtually every country in the world; all civil and military uses of nuclear energy; and a detailed accounting of all existing nuclear weapons, components, means of production, and stocks of fissile materials. The overall commitment of resources would be immense. There would also have to be a mechanism for dealing with violators, which would exceed any authority the world has yet granted to international organizations. The extent of this challenge is exemplified by the fact that although the UN has accorded itself unprecedented intrusion into the sovereignty of Iraq, after eight years it has been unable to certify that it has located all of Baghdad's facilities for producing weapons of mass destruction. Even advocates acknowledge that nuclear disarmament will require fundamental changes in the relations among nations. Still, there has clearly been amazing progress with respect to intrusive inspections and infringement into sovereignties during the past several decades. Advocates of disarmament argue that these trends are likely to accelerate with experience. One of the most prestigious advocacy groups is the Canberra Commission on the Elimination of Nuclear Weapons, which was convened during 1995–1996 by the Australian government. It stated the case for zero thus: "Nuclear weapons are held by a handful of states which insist that these weapons provide unique security benefits, and yet reserve uniquely to themselves the right to own them. This situation is highly discriminatory and thus unstable; it cannot be sustained. The possession of nuclear weapons by a state is a constant stimulus to other states to acquire them."[1] It is quite logical to conclude that if a few nations have nuclear weapons and most do not, then some nonnuclear nations would try to get them. If nuclear weapons are useful for some, they almost certainly must be for others also. Going to zero wold eliminate that element of instability but would incite another: If no one ostensibly possesses nuclear weapons, the potential leverage from being the only one in the world with them would appear to be enormous. One day we must decide whether the chances of proliferation are greater if no one has nuclear weapons or if a few do. This, though, is not a matter that begs for immediate resolution. In the meantime we need to recognize that the goal of getting safely to zero is so distant and problematic that it is difficult to generate public enthusiasm for it. To get the American public interested, we need a goal that appears more achievable.

One that is drawing increasing attention is the dealerting of nuclear forces. This ranges from turning off switches in the command system to removing guidance components from missiles to taking warheads off missiles or away from aircraft. One impediment is that in most cases detailed treaties, with attendant delays, would be needed to provide for verification. We could, though, afford to dealert a good many forces unilaterally while watching to see if the Russians were following suit. Dealerting, then, should be pursued as far as is practicable without treaties and, where treaties are necessary, as soon as they can be negotiated.

Still another option for supplementing the treaty process is to pursue more vigorously the triad of initiatives proposed earlier: strategic escrow, a pledge of no first-use, and modest defenses. The most logical way to expand these initiatives would be to incorporate as many additional nations as possible. For instance, with respect to strategic escrow, it would include inviting any nation adhering to the NPT, BWC, and CWC to provide observers at the escrow storage sites for nuclear, biological, and chemical weapons. The primary objective would be to build confidence that the weapons truly were being immobilized. Involving nonnuclear nations in the process would also demonstrate a wide interest in ensuring that all countries with weapons of mass destruction get them all into escrow.

And were Russia to balk at going too far into escrow, these other powers would be in position to encourage them to do so. Third parties could, hopefully, convince the Russians how desperately they need this program in the nuclear field.[2] With escrow, Russia and the United States together would step down the readiness of nuclear forces; without it the Russian forces would continue to decline unilaterally. As an additional inducement, an international group could even offer the Russians a monetary reward, say, a million dollars, for each warhead placed in escrow. Such an incentive might just flush out warheads not in the Russian accounting system. The United States could contribute to a warhead fund, but if we were the sole participant the Russians might suspect us of reaching for a military advantage.

With respect to the second initiative—a pledge of no nuclear first-use—a major new initiative would be to expand such a pledge into a Treaty of No First-Use (NFU) destruction. The obligations of such a treaty would be to renounce the first-use of nuclear, biological, and chemical weapons; to agree to share intelligence on nations and groups seeking to acquire and/or use such weapons; and to endorse making any first use of any weapon of mass destruction a crime against humanity. One hundred seventy-nine of the 185 signatories to the NPT are nonnuclear powers, which pledge not to acquire nuclear weapons. They should, therefore, have little reason to balk at agreeing not to use them first. Similarly, 140 nations have forsaken first-use of biological weapons in ratifying the BWC, 169 the first-use of chemical weapons in the CWC. A few nations might be concerned with the possibility of having to condemn a close ally that employed a weapon of mass destruction, but in signing the treaty they would be agreeing only to a generalized case, not one pointed at any particular nation.

Nations that did not sign the NFU would be suspects to be watched closely. The international consensus behind the NFU would warn any rogue nation of the risks in employing any of these weapons. One could hope such a treaty could even lead to agreement to impose sanctions against *any* user of a weapon of mass destruction or *any* state that was the base for terrorists that employ them. Sanctions are, after all, an accepted, if controversial, device for controlling international behavior. The UN has employed them against Iraq since the end of the Gulf War in 1991 and against Libya since 1992. The United States has also used them unilaterally in attempting to curtail nuclear proliferation. Still, some nations fear the use of sanctions could set a precedent to be used against them later; others refuse to subordinate their commercial relations to the sanctions; others object that economic sanctions often hurt citizens more than their leaders and their country; and others argue that it is difficult to terminate sanctions. If sanctions were used for important purposes, such as deterring aggression with weapons of mass destruction, such concerns would carry less weight. The core list of potential sanctions should include:

- Severance of diplomatic ties.
- Suspension of membership in the United Nations.
- Denying admission of the aggressor's aircraft and ships to territorial airspaces and waters.
- Freezing all governmental and private assets within reach.
- Indictment of the nation or group and its leaders for perpetrating a crime against humanity, as stipulated in the NFU. This provision would supersede the 1996 opinion of the International Court of Justice that first-use of nuclear weapons can be tolerated in exceptional circumstances.
- Stopping all economic activity with the aggressor, including the severance of as much electronic and mail communication as possible, halting the delivery of all commercial products, and prohibiting the transfer of armaments.
- Secondary sanctions against those who deliberately thwart the primary sanctions.
- The use of multinational conventional military forces to establish air and sea blockades for the purpose of enforcing the economic sanctions.
- Establishing a multinational extradition treaty that would authorize the arrest of any person declared as related to the aggressor's outlawed activities.

- Deployment of multinational military forces to countries neighboring the aggressor nation to deter military assaults.
- The use of conventional military forces to remove the aggressor's government and capture its leadership.

Nations would be allowed to sign on only to the specific sanctions they could accept and enforce. If there were not too many exceptions, these sanctions would cripple any nation subjected to them. Even if only the major powers presented a concerted front, it would be very intimidating. How diligent the signatory states would be in actually applying the sanctions once invoked is uncertain and would vary with the particular circumstance. The most important point is whether would-be aggressors with weapons of mass destruction believed the sanctions would be sufficiently enforced to be crippling. Each aggressor would evaluate that prospect differently, but the substantial risk in using weapons of mass destruction would be clear to all.

The concern that sanctions can be difficult to terminate could be explicitly addressed in treaty provisions stipulating the terms for termination: (1) the capture and trial of the leaders responsible before an International Criminal Court; (2) reparations being assessed by such an International Criminal Court; and (3) the indefinite installation of inspection and control mechanisms to prevent further development and maintenance of weapons of mass destruction.

One of the most attractive features of such a treaty would be its impact on terrorists. Even though they have no territory to threaten, the demonstration of international resolve would be sobering even to them. So, too, would the practical steps of sharing intelligence, threatening states that harbor terrorists who employ weapons of mass destruction, and promising international prosecution. Moreover, states harboring and supporting terrorists would have to consider the risk of being brought under sanctions.

Responsibility for organizing a Treaty of No First-Use falls to the United States. It would need to be done through an ad hoc process, since procedures for drafting treaties in the UN Conference on Disarmament almost always require unanimity, something difficult to obtain within a reasonable period. Ideally, the UN Security Council should administer the treaty, but there it would be subject to the veto power, risking that its purpose would be subverted. A three-phase progression thus seems necessary.

First: The United States pledges no first-use and promises unilateral sanctions and military actions in the event of aggression with weapons of mass destruction. Second: The United States negotiates adherence of as many nations as possible to a formal NFU, to be followed by a separate agreement on sanctions and the subsequent construction of an administrative mechanism for managing both treaty and sanctions. Third: The signatories transfer the treaty and the administrative mechanism to the UN after arranging for exemption from the veto power of the UN Security Council's permanent members.

Embarking on such a course would entail risks, such as involvement of the United States in conflicts to which we were not a party. That is unavoidable, at least with nuclear weapons. If nuclear weapons were used anywhere, the United States would inevitably be the dominant force in bringing the conflict to a halt and in taking steps to prevent recurrence. Failure on our part to play such a role would encourage the use of nuclear weapons in future conflicts and terrorist actions. We must, though, get our own house in order first by renouncing first-use and then encouraging our friends to understand that: (1) We believe that through diplomacy and conventional military preparedness they can ensure their own security; (2) we would help them do that and thus avoid their being placed in a position where resort to nuclear weapons seemed necessary; and (3) in the event of their employing these weapons we would take the side of the greater interests of humankind—condemning any use of them. In brief, we should let the world know that we are resolutely opposed to anyone initiating the use of weapons of mass destruction.* We have long pledged to allies that we would come to their aid should they become the victims of nuclear attack. This new formulation would expand that assurance to any victim—a universal guarantee of punishment for nuclear aggression, using whatever means are appropriate.

The third part of the triad is modest defenses. A valuable move here would be to offer the technology for defenses against weapons of mass destruction to any nation we consider responsible and that has reason to feel

---

*Today, such a policy is not politically realistic, especially in the event of Israel's using a nuclear weapon to defend itself against a conventional assault. After all, if we espouse the use of nuclear weapons to defend our European allies against conventional attacks, we could hardly deny Israel, or anyone else, the same right.

vulnerable. Most specifically these would be allies like Japan, South Korea, and Taiwan who feel exposed to China and North Korea; our NATO partners who could worry about accidental attacks from Russia; Israel, which would feel vulnerable if any Arab state acquired weapons of mass destruction; and Pakistan and India who, at the least, must worry about accidental attacks from the other. If there were actual proliferation of weapons of mass destruction, we would reassess whether additional countries should receive defensive assistance. Overall, we should offer defensive capabilities to those who want them in all but exceptional cases. The better defenses nations have, the less they are tempting targets for aggressors.

Significantly, the reinforcement of each element of the triad of initiatives involves incorporating many more nations in the process of preventing the proliferation or use of weapons of mass destruction. What we should aim for is a system of global management of these weapons that will make it unrewarding to use them. The most striking example of such a program is the mandates the United Nations enacted in 1991 prohibiting Iraq from having any weapons of mass destruction or the capability for manufacturing them. It is not unprecedented for a vanquished nation to be subjected to restraints. However, it is unprecedented to have the world community impose them. It is not surprising, then, that there is controversy surrounding how to enforce these mandates. However this issue is ultimately resolved, we should keep in mind that those UN mandates are an indicator that the world community is firmly opposed to the possession of any weapons of mass destruction by this one nation. There are other aggressive nations the world community should also want to see denied these weapons. The mandates on Iraq should be viewed as a precedent for more vigorous international actions to contain nuclear, biological, and chemical weapons. This points us, in my opinion, inexorably toward a startling new objective in the global management of weapons of mass destruction: Nations will be required either to comply with the international agreements on these weapons—the NPT, BWC, and CWC—or be forced to do so by the United Nations through devices such as sanctions and military action. This objective will not be achieved easily or quickly (witness Iraq's fierce resistance to intrusive inspections and supervised dismantlement of prohibited materials). Iraq is an example, though, that when nuclear, biological, and chemical weapons appear to be sufficiently threatening, the world community can develop the cohesion and cooperation needed to manage the problem.

In the meantime, there are activities to discourage the proliferation of weapons of mass destruction that deserve support. Almost all require strong international cooperation:

- International intelligence sharing—It is never easy to persuade intelligence agencies to share information with other countries when that information could identify their sources of information. Changing that could only be accomplished by direction from the highest political authorities. Appeal can be made, however, that weapons of mass destruction are of great common interest and that it is unlikely sufficient data could be collected by any one intelligence organization. Mostly, what is needed is for intelligence organizations to identify and share the clues for which everyone should be watching. Next in importance is having a central point for bringing the data together and interpreting it. That would have to be a special U.S. unit that could tap the wide range of resources of the U.S. intelligence community. For instance, if the seemingly innocent movement of a Russian biologist to Iraq gets reported into the system, it would be compared in the U.S. unit with another innocent report about an order placed in Germany by an Iraqi firm for biological fermentation equipment; the unit could then request several additional appropriate intelligence organizations to use these leads to look for more clues. In turn, the United States would need to share what it learns whenever possible so as to promote continuing cooperation.

- Controls on exports—The Nuclear Suppliers Group is a derivative of the Cold War mechanism for controlling the export of materials related to nuclear weapons to the Soviet bloc and China. It works closely with the Exporters (Zangger) Committee established under the NPT. These groups set worldwide standards for controlling the supply of materials that could contribute to nuclear proliferation. Another organization, the Australia Group (AG), was created in 1984 on the initiative of the Australian government to establish common export controls for biological and chemical materials. The thirty member countries* enact domestic legislation under which manufacturers must obtain approval for export of listed items such as manufacturing equipment, biological agents, various microorganisms, and precursor substances for the production of biological and chemical agents. The United States also imposes unilateral sanctions from time to time. In 1997 sanctions were imposed on several Chinese entities and one Hong Kong company for supplying dual-use chemical precursors to Iran; on a German citizen and a German company for exporting chemical production equipment to Libya; and on two Russian firms for dealings with Iran. All of these international and national mechanisms deserve continuing support.

- Safeguarding Russian nuclear materials—A number of bilateral and multilateral programs exist to improve the security surrounding Russian nuclear weapons and fissionable materials. The CTR Program was originally sponsored by Senators Sam Nunn and Richard Lugar in 1991 to assist the Russians in safeguarding, storing, and destroying weapons of mass destruction and the materials associated with them. The United States has appropriated something like $400 million per year for this effort. In 1994 the United States and Russia agreed on another program for dealing with highly enriched uranium accumulated as Russia dismantles nuclear weapons. The United States purchases and reprocesses the highly enriched uranium removed from Russian nuclear warheads and recycles it into reactor fuel. France, Canada, and Germany are scheduled to participate in this program by purchasing some of that fuel. Presidents Boris Yeltsin and Bill Clinton also agreed in September 1997 to reduce the stocks of plutonium the two countries hold by fifty tons.

---

*Argentina, Australia, Austria, Belgium, Britain, Canada, Czech Republic, Denmark, Finland, France, Germany, Greece, Hungary, Iceland, Ireland, Italy, Japan, Luxembourg, Netherlands, New Zealand, Norway, Poland, Romania, Slovak Republic, South Korea, Spain, Sweden, Switzerland, and the United States. They meet annually and produce updated lists of prohibited items for the member states to incorporate into their export restriction lists.

- Controls on Russian scientific talent—An offshoot of the CTR program is the International Science and Technology Center (ISTC) in Moscow, which began operations in Russia in 1994. Recognizing that there is a lack of funding for scientific research in Russia today, the ISTC funds the salaries of Russian scientists from the nuclear, biological, chemical, and missile fields. The objective is to dissuade them from taking their skills to countries seeking to acquire weapons of mass destruction by funding specific joint projects in peaceful areas such as the environment, manufacturing technology, nonnuclear energy sources, biotechnology, and life sciences. It concentrates on scientist-to-scientist contacts between the contributing countries and those of the former Soviet Union. It helps Russian scientists to understand the role of science in a free market economy and the dividends of open scientific research. It is a multinational intergovernmental organization funded by the United States, the European Union, Norway, South Korea, and Japan. Through mid-1998 almost 600 projects were funded at nearly $175 million, involving 21,000 former Soviet scientists at nearly 300 research institutions in Armenia, Belarus, Kazakhstan, and Ukraine. An effort is being made to make the ISTC commercially self-supporting. In the meantime, congressional funding for the U.S. share is, unfortunately, diminishing.
- Strengthening the BWC—One hundred forty nations have ratified the BWC. Four BWC Review Conferences since 1994 and a continuing Ad Hoc Group have failed, however, to develop acceptable mechanisms for verifying compliance. Agreement had been slow to develop on the definition of what biological production is authorized and what is not; on how much transparency, including surprise inspections, is required; and on how to protect proprietary commercial data from being stolen. The commonality of legitimate biological research and production with that for weapons, plus the small quantities involved, make resolving these issues very difficult. American policy appears to be less than fully committed. Apparently the feeling is that the Australia Group, the ISTC, and the CTR hold greater promise for constraining the proliferation of biological weapons. There are,

though, ways to surmount some of the problems of verification of the BWC. One would be to develop sampling techniques that can be read on the spot and discarded, so that inspectors do not take away samples that could reveal commercial secrets. Unfortunately, U.S. reluctance to strengthen the BWC seems to be a combination of bureaucratic inertia and strong influence from the $100 billion U.S. pharmaceutical industry. Concern about theft of commercial proprietary data in this rapidly moving field is genuine, but it can be largely mitigated by rules for managing access to facilities. And whatever risks there are for industry need to be placed in the larger perspective of curtailing biological warfare.

- Making the CWC work—One hundred sixty-nine nations have signed the CWC. Russia, with its huge stockpiles of these weapons, needs more financial assistance and encouragement to eliminate them. For more than a year the United States failed to enact the necessary enabling legislation, then did so with reservations on challenge inspections, sampling techniques, and the scope of required disclosures. This was out of concern for the loss of proprietary data but may gravely reduce the treaty's usefulness. Here we must also assess the priority we want to accord to preventing proliferation.
- Controls on missiles—Since 1987 there has been an international Missile Technology Control Regime (MTCR) to limit exports in materials and components related to longer-range ballistic missiles. It has not been sufficiently successful. Of the key offenders, Russia and China have pledged closer adherence; North Korea has not. Every responsible nation has a stake in this regime; it deserves greater support.
- Removing causes of instability—If the root causes behind nuclear, biological, and chemical aggression could be eliminated, the problem of dealing with weapons of mass destruction will disappear. It is, of course, improbable that all such causes can be addressed to everyone's satisfaction. At present the impulses to acquire weapons of mass destruction stem primarily from nationalistic, religious, and ethnic grievances that are difficult to address (witness the delays with the peace process in the Middle East). When we look farther down the road, however, the growing

disparities in income around the world could well become a problem. These deserve to be addressed on humanitarian grounds alone, but we would do well to keep in mind that biological and chemical weapons in particular may be perceived by leaders of aggrieved nations to give them leverage over more powerful opponents.

The involvement of many nations in these myriad undertakings to limit proliferation is the key to success in controlling these weapons. It promotes an international norm that weapons of mass destruction are not to be considered weapons of warfare and are not to be employed. It opens the possibility of a system of global management to control these threats. Historically nations have seldom foresworn powerful weapons. But will the threat of weapons of mass destruction be perceived sufficiently grave to galvanize the world community in this direction? The stakes are high, not only because of the horrendous damage these weapons could do but also because establishing firm control over them could be a precedent for controlling lesser forms of violence as well. In the best of all worlds, we could even hope that an understanding of both the pragmatic and moral impediments to the use of weapons of mass destruction would gradually apply to conventional warfare as well. How many conventional wars have been fought to achieve objectives that simply were not achievable through the use of force? How much of the world's wealth has gone into armaments that were in excess of any legitimate need? There is a long tradition of attempting to curtail the most egregious weapons, such as the French-German treaty of 1675 outlawing poisoned bullets. Could it even be that in time controls on weapons will be applied to progressively lesser forms of violence, until violence among nations is removed from the world's agenda?

Partly because it was we who introduced nuclear weapons, the United States must shoulder the responsibility of leading the world into a system of global management for weapons of mass destruction. In addition, we are the only nation with the combination of conscience and wherewithal to undertake such a responsibility. After World War II, the United States designed and implemented the Marshall Plan. We looked also at a plan to establish international control over all aspects of the use of nuclear energy but did not manage that partly because the Cold War was upon us. Now that the Cold War is over, we are in a position to lead the world in that direction. In order to lead we must be in front. That means, for instance, not just making a single effort at strategic escrow but, if the Russians do not follow immediately, several. That means pledging not only no first-use but also being willing to punish aggressors using weapons of mass destruction, even before a treaty can be negotiated. That means passing domestic legislation to comply with the CWC and negotiating aggressively to establish verification routines under the BWC. That means boldly sharing the technologies of strategic defenses against ballistic missiles. It is one thing to suggest the world needs a strong norm against weapons of mass destruction. It is another to take bold steps in that direction.

If we have that vision, we can cage the nuclear, biological, and chemical genies.

9

RESHAPING DECISIONMAKING

IN JUNE 1979, PRESIDENT JIMMY CARTER called a meeting of the National Security Council to decide whether or not to ask Congress to fund the development of the MX ballistic missile system. The president normally called upon me as Director of Central Intelligence to open such meetings by presenting relevant intelligence data. It was not my province to suggest what the president should decide, lest that appear to prejudice my appraisal of the facts. There were times, however, that it was very difficult not to get involved in the heart of the discussion. This was one of those instances. What I did was to offer an analysis of what the Soviet response would be if we built the MX and fielded it using the forty-three shelter "racetrack" scheme. This was close to offering an opinion that the basing plan was bizarre and the MX was unnecessary.

The conclusion in the CIA was that the Soviets would counter our deployment of the MX in some way. We expected their reaction to be similar to what ours would be: Threaten as much of the opponent's military force as possible. We decided they would aim one warhead at each of the forty-three moderately hardened shelters on the racetracks, rather than attempt to discern which shelter actually contained the missile. They would have enough warheads under SALT II, which we were then negotiating, to do that. Thus, the effect of creating forty-three shelters for each MX, rather than placing them in standard, vulnerable ICBM silos, would be to invite more nuclear detonations on our soil in the event of nuclear war.

There was no rebuttal to this line of reasoning from those present representing military interests, the secretary of defense, and the chairman of the Joint Chiefs of Staff, or even from Zbig Brzezinski, who favored the MX. They simply shifted the discussion to whether the president should select a large- or moderate-size version of the missile. My opinion was that the smaller MX was decidedly preferable because we would have the option of making it modestly mobile, and hence less vulnerable, by mounting it on a truck trailer, a railroad car, or an aircraft. What our military clearly wanted was the most powerful counterweight to the even larger ICBMs on the Soviet side. The unspoken argument favoring the larger missile, however, was that nothing less would placate those senators who were wavering on whether to ratify SALT II. It was going to be nip and tuck to garner the sixty-seven votes necessary for approval. The president had to hook some of the senators who were in doubt, and the MX was the bait.

As the meeting drew to a close, President Carter said, in effect, "As I understand the discussion, everyone agrees we should proceed with the MX and in the larger version." I raised my hand: "Mr. President, it is not my role to comment on policy issues, but your use of 'everyone' included me. I do not agree." Not unexpectedly, this had no effect.

CHANGING THE UNDERLYING PREMISES of our nuclear policies as fundamentally as I have suggested would require dedicated leadership by the U.S. president and Congress alike. We have aspired in the past to similarly dramatic changes but have always failed. In 1946 we submitted the Acheson-Lilienthal/Baruch plan to the United Nations for international control over nuclear technology, either for weapons or energy, the end objective being to dispense with nuclear weapons entirely. The Soviet Union thought this was a guise for perpetuating U.S. nuclear hegemony, and the plan was killed almost the moment it was submitted. In 1986 in Reykjavik, Iceland, Ronald Reagan and Mikhail Gorbachev, working without advisers, almost agreed to eliminate either all ballistic missiles (the U.S. proposal) or all strategic nuclear weapons (the Soviet proposal) within ten years. This startling breakthrough foundered on differences over strategic defenses.

The question today is whether these precedents suggest we should proceed cautiously toward similarly revolutionary changes or, with the end of the Cold War, whether we should hold out for even greater change. In my view, the forces of resistance are sufficiently in retreat that a firm commitment from a president could move us forward aggressively. Moreover, to proceed piecemeal would only play into the hands of those who will seek to slow the process at every stage.

Surprisingly, however, presidents have not played decisive roles in deciding numbers of nuclear weapons or plans for targeting them, although they certainly knew that the numbers in our arsenal and the amount of damage designed into our war plans were excessive. We can surmise a number of reasons for their reluctance to grapple directly with these wasteful and risky practices. One is that mastering nuclear terminology and technology is time consuming. It also requires perseverance, because military officers are always reluctant to involve civilians in war plans—conventional or nuclear—lest the civilians tinker without possessing adequate expertise. That feeling has been especially strong with nuclear plans because they have been considered so essential to the nation's security.

Early in the nuclear era, this aversion to outside interference bordered on insubordination. General Curtis LeMay, commander of the Strategic Air Command from 1948 to 1957, felt so strongly that only he and his experts could formulate our nuclear strategic plans that for several years he failed to inform even the Joint Chiefs of Staff of changes he had made to those plans.[1] LeMay was an extremist, but his reluctance to share information on nuclear war plans persisted. Beginning with Robert McNamara in 1961, secretaries of defense intruded more and more into this military province, but presidential involvement still was limited. For instance, until the early 1970s the Joint Chiefs of Staff did not brief any president on their annual nuclear war game, which estimated the outcome of a nuclear exchange with the Soviet Union, and then did so largely because they believed the results would justify requests for more nuclear weapons.[2] During the late 1970s, President Carter made a diligent, personal effort to understand our nuclear position. By 1989 the balance had tipped sufficiently that President George Bush, through Secretary of Defense Dick Cheney, put his hand directly on the targeting situation, eliminating thousands of unnecessary targets. And in 1991 President Bush unilaterally withdrew almost all tactical nuclear weapons from deployed positions.

One reason this process took so long is that it has been neither necessary nor advantageous for a president to stir up the issue of reducing numbers of nuclear weapons. It was not necessary because all had confidence that they could control *any* release of nuclear weapons, no matter how many we had. Also, there was no political advantage to taking on the issue, only the risk of being painted as soft on communism and of challenging the proclivities of the military and military-industrial complex for more and more weapons. For example, President Carter's task of persuading the Senate to ratify SALT II would have been impossible had the Joint Chiefs of Staff opposed the treaty.

To get numbers under control despite the military's thirst for more weapons, all presidents since John Kennedy have turned more to arms control agreements with the Soviet Union and Russia rather than to internal reforms. At first these agreements constrained growth in the two arsenals, but later they led to reduced numbers and to actions to avoid accidental, unauthorized, and miscalculated use. The public has accepted the idea that continuing reductions is the norm. For instance, unilateral moves by Presidents Bush and Clinton to reduce the risk of accidents were accepted as a matter of fact. What this means, I believe, is that additional presidential initiatives to curtail reliance on nuclear weapons could be well received. In the long run, progress in this direction could stand out as a president's mark for posterity—the enduring impact on humanity of reducing the risk of nuclear devastation.

To effect substantial change in nuclear policies, a president would have to reshape the bureaucracies to overcome strong bureaucratic dedication to the traditional precepts of nuclear strategy. Most of those precepts— for example, more is always better—have never been sound. The fact that they persisted throughout the entire Cold War gives the false appearance of validity. A president, then, would do well to break down the current bureaucratic system, which still is heavily influenced by those precepts. To appreciate why this is a problem, we need to return to Clausewitz's dictum that war is a continuation of policy by other means, that is, that the nation's political aims govern decisions on preparing for and conducting war.

Clausewitz, however, was vague on just how to divide those decisions between political and military authorities: He said that "operational details like the posting of guards or the employment of patrols" should not be a matter for political decision.[3] That is adequate advice at the lower, tactical end of the spectrum of military decisionmaking. As we move toward the higher, strategic end, however, we need to elaborate on Clausewitz, because political factors become increasingly important. Thus, we need a new maxim: *Any military decision with significant implications for policy must be based on significant guidance from political authorities.* When it comes to nuclear weapons, almost every decision in peace or war fits that formula. For example: The numbers and types of nuclear weapons in our arsenal threaten others in a way no amount of conventional weaponry could; the doctrine enunciated for using them signals a frightening intent; and any use of even one nuclear weapon after a half-century tradition of nonuse would have untold implications for humankind.

This is not to say there has not been a shift away from the dominant role the military played in nuclear strategy under General LeMay. Our decision process does place control of all decisions on nuclear weapons in the hands of civilian policymakers, and they are exercising that authority more today than even ten years ago. Specific targets are proposed by the commander in chief of the Strategic Command in Omaha based on broad objectives set out by the secretary of defense. Recommended targets are then approved or disapproved by the secretary. The Strategic Command, however, is inclined to favor military targets and ways to gain favorable exchange ratios.

Although these are not necessarily bad practices for winning conventional wars, "winning" a nuclear war is quite a different matter. At the upper extreme, if we were pushed past our point of non-recovery, there could be no victor. Our objective in retaliating would be to push the opponent past its point of non-recovery also. That would not be a matter of exchange ratios or numbers of targets destroyed but of an imprecise amount of societal and economic disruption that cumulatively would bring that society to a prolonged halt. At the lower end, say, a limited nuclear attack, the success of our retaliation would still not be measured in amounts of destruction but in whether the enemy understood from our controlled response that the consequences of continuing would be more disastrous than capitulation.

Between these two extremes—limited, demonstrative controlled response and the societal destruction of non-recovery—there are various levels of nuclear exchanges. Nowhere on that spectrum is the amount of physical destruction the appropriate criterion. Rather, since we would lose more with every exchange, our measure of success should be the earliest termination on favorable terms. How we use force to bring that about is not a military matter but a political judgment. All across the spectrum, then, from very controlled to very wide nuclear responses, the desired effects are measured in political terms more than military—not in how much is destroyed but in how quickly the opponent understands that policy objectives cannot be fulfilled by continuing to wage nuclear war. It is neither wise nor fair to charge *military* planners with drawing up plans tailored primarily to *political* concerns. The last thing we should want is to encourage the military to set the political objectives of war.

How could we revamp our decision process to take better account of policy objectives? The locus for selecting targets, weapons, and delivery vehicles could be shifted even more toward civilian policymakers in the Department of Defense. For instance, targets intended for controlled responses should be selected by those who best understand the culture, psychology, and personal factors influencing specific foreign leaders and leadership elites; targets intended to push an opponent past non-recovery should be selected on the basis of analyses of economic and societal effects by those with such expertise. In the past, given the thousands upon thousands of targets and the requirement for precisely timing the arrival of warheads, it took the immense computer capabilities at the Strategic Command to pull together a million pages of war plans. But if we are talking about only 250 targets (enough to cause the non-recovery of Russia and China, more than enough as to other countries of concern), the problem is more manageable.

The Strategic Command still needs to be intimately involved, but only in certifying with what probability and accuracy it can deliver weapons to assigned targets. The end product would be a menu of options—selected by civilian policymakers and vetted by the Strategic Command—from which any president could choose according to the circumstances. In recent years, the Department of Defense has been moving in this direction by creating more options within set war plans. Despite these, our doctrine for using nuclear weapons to achieve favorable exchange ratios and our sense of urgency to respond before more of our own forces are attacked have made it likely that a president would be pressured into a set war plan with a large number of nuclear weapons. We need to escape the burden of preset plans altogether, especially those calling for massive response. Presidents should construct their own war plans from menus of options they and their advisers have created in advance.

By asking policymakers to play an even larger role in selecting targets there is a danger of merely handing authority from one bureaucracy to another, one that might be equally disposed to the traditional precepts of nuclear strategy. After all, civilian experts on nuclear strategy developed many of these questionable precepts in the first place. To avoid this, any civilian authorities who develop targeting menus must reflect the policy views of the president. One way to ensure this is to create a second, presidentially appointed position of deputy secretary of defense, exclusively for nuclear security. This would effectively divide the Pentagon into nuclear and nonnuclear sides. Only the Joint Chiefs of Staff and various support elements would be on both sides. There would, of course, be areas of overlap, for example, attack submarines and strategic bombers with both conventional and nuclear missions. Overlap problems are manageable by establishing ground rules. For example, a commander of attack submarines with a conventional mission would not be allowed to remove nuclear weapons from them or send them out of their assigned theaters without permission from the deputy secretary of defense for nuclear security; a commander of strategic bombers would not be allowed to send them on a conventional mission without the agreement of the deputy secretary. It would also be useful to consolidate a single budget for all nuclear forces under this deputy secretary rather than put pieces in the budgets of the military services, as at present. The tradeoffs between nuclear and conventional forces should be at this higher level, because under a policy of no first-use they are not interchangeable.

Overall, such a realignment of responsibilities would drive home two points: that we would never introduce nuclear weapons into a conventional war, even as a last resort; and that in the event of being forced to use nuclear weapons in retaliation to a nuclear attack we would not automatically resort to traditional rules for fighting but would use controlled responses under the direction of civilian policymakers. One hopes that having a presidential appointee with no responsibilities other than nuclear matters would not only ensure that the president's views were accurately reflected in policies and actions but also encourage greater presidential involvement in the entire decision process.

A president seeking to instill a new philosophy as to nuclear weapons would also do well to establish a system of checks from outside the Department of Defense. Bureaucratic organizations are not only resistant to change but also expert at stifling imaginative ideas and dissenting views. Moreover, decisions on nuclear forces, policies, and uses are so important that a president should hear several points of view, including those of people who have no bureaucratic axes to grind. One way to get such wide-ranging advice to a president would be to create a Presidential Council for Nuclear Security composed of seven individuals from outside the government serving part-time expressly for this purpose, plus the secretaries of defense, state, and energy; the head of the Arms Control and Disarmament Agency; the chairman of the Joint Chiefs of Staff; and the Director of Central Intelligence.

These thirteen—six insiders plus seven outsiders including the chair—would constitute the president's top advisory body on all decisions concerning nuclear weapons: procurement, targeting plans, peacetime deployment, and wartime operations. They would act much as a corporate board of directors, with a mix of insiders with detailed knowledge and outsiders with more detached objectivity. The council would have a modest staff to do fact-finding independently of the bureaucracies. It would enjoy access to all information on nuclear matters and would attempt to ensure that the president's policies were, in fact, being carried out. The body would meet periodically with the National Security Council to ensure that nuclear policy was in harmony with other military and political policies. During a potential nuclear crisis, the Council for Nuclear Security and the National Security Council would meet jointly to advise the president.

These three steps—shifting targeting decisions to policymakers, creating the position of deputy secretary of defense for nuclear security, and establishing the Council for Nuclear Security—would accentuate the role that civilian advisers play over military advisers. Giving greater responsibility to civilian policymakers in formulating nuclear strategy can be justified only by the fact that political factors dominate military ones, that is, decisions must be based more on political appraisal than on military technique. The downside is that military advice is usually professional and consistent, whereas advice from a largely civilian council—especially one with a majority of nongovernment members—would likely fluctuate. Members would come and go, and the outsiders especially would need time to gain experience and expertise. The upside is that political policies deserve periodic reexamination, more so than military strategies, because there are fewer certainties, as for example weapons performance data and standard tactics. A president, in selecting outside members, would want to strike a balance between those with established opinions and expertise in nuclear matters and those unfamiliar with the issues but with very inquiring minds. Most should share the president's basic philosophies on nuclear policies, but some should represent sufficiently differing views to give the council respectability in the eyes of the American public.

An additional step would be to return to the earlier practice of assigning custody of all nuclear warheads to the Department of Energy. In the majority of cases, this would be nominal, as the Department of Energy would have to suballocate warheads actually deployed in operational units to the Department of Defense. Energy, however, would be entitled to oversee the controls on those warheads, for example, the number in each silo, submarine, and storage bunker on strategic bomber bases. Energy would also assume physical custody of all warheads not deployed with an operational unit, including excess units awaiting dismantling, units in transit, and units being used for reliability inspections. This practice would help establish the principle that nuclear weapons are not military property to be employed in war-fighting.

The president would need support from Congress to implement these initiatives. Congressional involvement in nuclear issues began with the formation of the Joint Committee on Atomic Energy in 1942; it was very active initially but disbanded in 1977. Congressional jurisdiction over nuclear weapons was assumed by the House and Senate committees on armed services, which have created subcommittees on nuclear matters. Their roles have been more of supervisory observation than of positive direction. The issues are complex, there is minimal constituent interest in the topic, and there always loomed the risk of being painted as soft on communism. The end of the Cold War mitigates the last factor, but the other two remain problematic for members.

Another point to consider when discussing the role of Congress is the pressure members receive from the military-industrial lobby to build more expensive nuclear delivery systems, like bombers and submarines. With nuclear force levels clearly on the decline, there will be less of this pressure. In any event, Congress traditionally has insisted that we keep pace with the Soviets in terms of numbers; whether this will continue in regard to the Russians is difficult to forecast. The composition of Congress is changing. More than half of the members in the Senate and two-thirds in the House have never served in the military; in the 1996 and 1998 electoral campaigns, defense issues did not figure prominently. We must have hope that a few leaders in each chamber will encourage adequate attention to the reshaping of U.S. nuclear policy.

To stimulate reform, Congress could establish separate committees on nuclear security, something not very different from having subcommittees. But creating full committees would accentuate the philosophy that nuclear weapons are more political instruments than military ones. There would be a clear risk, however, of seeing these committees become bastions of support for more nuclear weapons, as was the case with the Joint Committee on Atomic Energy. In my view, that is a risk we should take: The elected representatives of the people must be active and full participants in decisions as vital as those on nuclear matters.

In addition, Congress should appropriate all funds for procuring and maintaining nuclear weapons to a single department. Currently, appropriations for the Department of Energy cover laboratory research, development, testing, and production of nuclear weapons; those for the Department of Defense cover all operational aspects. Over the years, this division has had the insidious effect of encouraging the Department of Defense to be somewhat cavalier about asking for more and different kinds of nuclear weapons, as it has not had to pay for developing and producing them. The more practical solution would be to consolidate all these moneys in the defense budget. Defense would, then, reimburse the Department of Energy for services rendered. The opposite solution—putting everything in the energy budget—would have the merit of emphasizing the nonmilitary role of nuclear weapons, but it would likely be unacceptable to the Department of Defense.

Evolutionary changes in established bureaucratic processes simply become absorbed. Revolutionary change, because it is unsettling, can throw the bureaucrats off base just long enough to give the changes a chance to survive.

10

THE SINE QUA NON— CITIZEN SUPPORT

IN JULY 1995, IN THE COURSE OF DOING RESEARCH for this book, I visited the Strategic Command at Offutt Air Force Base outside Omaha, Nebraska. My key objective was to see how nuclear policy had changed since my last visit, in 1980 as Director of Central Intelligence. Back then, I was comparing the views at Offutt as to the balance of strategic forces with those at the CIA. They were pretty much in line, that is, the Soviets were improving their strategic nuclear forces and could well tip the balance in their favor, leaving us vulnerable to a preemptive attack; we needed to maintain parity so as to be able to "cover" all the targets that Soviet strategic forces presented.

An analysis, to which I subscribed, showing there was no possible window of vulnerability had not been accepted by the experts at CIA, and certainly not at Offutt. That analysis depended heavily on the assumption that U.S. SSBNs were quite invulnerable. I could see why that was an unpopular view at Offutt. The general on whom I called commanded the Strategic Air Command, an Air Force command with ICBMs and bombers. The other strategic nuclear force, Navy SSBNs, was controlled from Norfolk, Virginia, by an admiral. There was a rear admiral stationed at Offutt to ensure coordination of the two forces. It was this overall, coordinated posture that interested me, but my arranged schedule did not include a visit with the admiral and his staff. SAC was a proud, parochial command. I went away, however, wondering if the unique capabilities of

SSBNs were being adequately considered, for example, how there possibly could be a window of vulnerability.

When I returned fifteen years later, I knew important changes had been made. In 1992, SAC was abolished in favor of the Strategic Command, which incorporated operational control of Navy SSBNs with Air Force ICBMs and bombers. Accordingly, StratCom is to be commanded alternately by an Air Force general and a Navy admiral. All this seemed to be considerable progress. The man who had been a moving force behind this change, Air Force General Lee Butler, had retired but was living in Omaha. While in town I called on him. As mentioned earlier, when he first arrived he found some 12,000-plus targets among the million pages of war plans. He and his superiors in the Pentagon eliminated 75 percent of them—a prodigious accomplishment. He mentioned he had dropped many bridges from the target list, and I assumed the Bulgarian railroad bridge that first piqued my interest in nuclear targeting was among them.

I knew also of the growing ferment outside StratCom among prominent civilians and retired generals and admirals: former Secretary of Defense Robert S. McNamara; former Deputy Secretary of Defense Paul H. Nitze; General Butler; former Supreme Allied Commander in Europe General Andrew J. Goodpaster; and former commander of the U.S. Space Command General Charles Horner. These and more were sounding the alarm over the excessive numbers of nuclear weapons—not only in our arsenal but in others as well.*

The fact that Butler, Goodpaster, and Horner were involved in this was particularly significant to me. They had been direct participants in nuclear policy and yet had come to this conclusion. Surprisingly, at least to those outside the military, very few senior military officers have much understanding of nuclear strategy or any interest in it. (Remember that I was already a rear admiral when I first learned how shockingly many warheads were in the SIOP.) A small club of zealous military experts has dominated the military's input on nuclear weapons policy. The members of this club have insisted on parity with Russia, on being ready to fight it out even with large numbers of weapons, and on agonizing over a win-

---

*In December 1996, some sixty retired admirals and generals from fourteen countries (including nineteen from the United States, eighteen from Russia, four from the United Kingdom, and one from France) banded together and signed a manifesto recommending nuclear disarmament.

dow of vulnerability. As recently as 1994, they successfully twisted the Nuclear Posture Review into a meaningless effort.

As I went into the briefing room at StratCom on my return visit, I wondered where these people stood between the new thinking of Generals Butler, Goodpaster, and Horner and the old thinking of General LeMay. It was quickly obvious: Comparative numbers still mattered very much, although the fixation was weaker than it had been in 1980. The START II level of 3,500 warheads was a bare minimum to "cover" what we needed to cover; we could tolerate going down to 3,500 only if we held a reserve that allowed us to build back up. Despite the economic malaise within Russia, the officials at StratCom suspected the Russians were surreptitiously diverting resources to new nuclear capabilities. In answering my specific question, they did not think 3,500 warheads could bring Russia to its knees, that is, to its point of non-recovery, because it is such a large country. Their calculations took into account only the individual targets destroyed, for example, a factory, a military headquarters, or an ICBM silo—and did not account for the impact on the other elements of the society and economy of losing these services. They had never heard of the MIT study that showed that 250 warheads targeted on U.S. liquid fuel supplies could carry our country to non-recovery.

The responsibility of StratCom was to meet the broad criteria for targeting set down by the secretary of defense, for example, to destroy some percentage of all industry or of all ICBMs with high assurance. What the total effect on Russia would be was beyond their concern. As the meeting went on I asked, provocatively, "What if we would only target key points in the Russian industrial system, even if they were in cities—could we not do with a lot fewer weapons?" An officer was instantly dispatched with instructions to bring the command's legal officer to join us. He explained that targeting innocent civilians in cities was against international law. The generals in the room chimed in for good measure that the American public would not stand for such a targeting plan. The legal officer then was forthright in completing the picture: If our cities were attacked first, the law sanctioned retaliation in kind. The nuance, apparently, was that in peacetime it was illegal to draw up plans to target civilians, which left military targets or the sophistry that something like a power plant in the middle of a city did not involve innocent civilians. But if the Russians attacked first and hit our cities—as would be almost inevitable—well, then, all bets were off. Since I could not imagine the United States starting a nuclear war with Russia, it looked like the legal point was an academic excuse to help justify larger forces. It also fit General LeMay's thesis that we might go first.

I left feeling that despite all the changes that had taken place since Curtis LeMay left SAC in 1957, his influence on StratCom was much stronger than was Lee Butler's.

SECRECY IN A DEMOCRATIC GOVERNMENT IS ANATHEMA. This applies to the necessary secrecy of intelligence operations, to military war plans and equipment, to illegal or improper activities of the government itself—and to nuclear strategy. Nowhere in our government has secrecy been more profound than with respect to nuclear weapons. The great emphasis on secrecy concerning the Manhattan Project back in 1942 was easy to understand. After all, we saw ourselves in a fight with Germany on which the fate of the free world hinged. This carried over into the Cold War. Information about nuclear weapons was one of the first to be secluded in a special compartment above "Top Secret" labeled "Restricted Data." Access can still be had only with a special permit. A similarly restrictive approach was applied to our programs for biological and chemical weapons when they were active. It carries over to today for much data on those programs.

A partial result of all of this compartmentation of information is that presidents and the Congress have played a less active role in formulating policies on weapons of mass destruction than on any other policy of comparable import and expense. Even within the military, access to information on these weapons has been severely restricted. Under these circumstances, it is no wonder citizens have not been well informed. Indeed, they have been misinformed. Many civilian and military experts who shaped policy on nuclear weapons simply lost focus in concocting sophistic theories that never made sense when first formulated, for example, the necessity of a TRIAD of nuclear forces and plans to escalate nuclear war until we dominated—no matter what the damage to our country. If ever scrutiny by the public was needed because scrutiny by the bureaucracy was so limited, this was it.

Today, adequate citizen input to policies concerning weapons of mass destruction is still lacking. It will take greater openness on the government's part to generate it. The excuse against public involvement continues to be secrecy. There are, though, only two sectors where secrecy on weapons of mass destruction remains necessary. One is our capabilities and intentions for retaliating to attacks with weapons of mass destruction. The other is advanced techniques for making such weapons. The basic equations are readily available, but we do not want other data that would simplify the task to reach the hands of would-be proliferators. Iraq, for instance, has been forced to follow some cumbersome processes for refining fissionable material in searching for a nuclear capability. Within these limits, we need to devise ways to involve our citizens more. One approach would be for the government to publish more information to help the public grasp the essential elements of weapons of mass destruction. For example:

- A guide to the lethality of these weapons could be produced in the language of nonexperts. This would require the government to acknowledge why and how it has historically underestimated the effects of nuclear weapons. Much the same would apply to explaining the wide variations, even within the government, in estimates of the effects of chemical and biological weapons.
- Data could be released on the problems others face in manufacturing weapons of mass destruction and the state of progress of various aspirant countries. There would be objections that releasing such data showing just how much we know about other countries could compromise our intelligence sources. This need not be the case, however. There are ways to conceal the origin of the data, even by deliberately distorting it by modest amounts.
- Information on the past, present, and future costs of U.S. programs for weapons of mass destruction. This would enable the public to place these programs in perspective with other national needs. This should include the costs of repairing damage to the environment.
- Perhaps most important of all, statistics could be released on the risks we have taken and are taking, especially data as to the number of deaths and the amount of destruction we estimated would be caused by our nuclear war plans at various points in the past. The public needs to understand the extremes to which we

went and that we should avoid in the future. It should also summarize the impact of what we believe the Soviet Union's key war plans against the United States would have been or, if the Russians would cooperate, their own estimates of such impact.

There is nothing unusual about this proposal. The government regularly releases highly polished, unclassified reports on what our military strategy is, how much it costs, and what opposition we face. The incentive for this, of course, is to make the case for the Defense Department budget. There is no such incentive for informing the public about weapons of mass destruction. Some department or agency should be assigned the responsibility, after coordinating with the other agencies involved, of providing the public as much information as possible. The culture of secrecy in the Department of Defense is too strong for it to be tasked with this. The Department of State lacked the necessary expertise until it recently absorbed the Arms Control and Disarmament Agency. That makes it a logical candidate. There are those, however, who contend that stimulating public debate on weapons of mass destruction would elevate their importance, frightening rather than reassuring citizens. Letting the government decide what citizens should know, other than on grounds of secrecy, however, would be a greater risk in our democracy.

Once the basic data are available, the government's resources for engaging the public in debate on it are awesome. They start, of course, with the president's involvement and commitment—speeches, remarks to the press, and requests to the Congress ranging from resolutions of national intent to new laws to the ratification of treaties. Once a president is engaged, many other resources will flow: speeches by other officials, conferences, videos, publications, and encouragement to private organizations.

The private sector also has almost endless opportunities for galvanizing public interest. The media naturally will key off speeches and press conferences. The more responsible leadership in the media will recognize the importance of a topic like weapons of mass destruction and encourage attention to it. And there are myriad private foundations, institutes, councils, and study groups, plus the writings of individuals. These all can contribute greatly to informing the public on weapons of mass destruction. Much attention in the private sector today has shifted from national security to domestic issues. This is understandable and in many ways justified.

The issues of peace and war still plague us, however, and the specter of weapons of mass destruction will not just go away. A well-informed public could help us escape from the senseless and outdated theorems of nuclear warfare, such as the importance of numerical parity, windows of vulnerability, and the possible utility of initiating nuclear war. A better understanding of the realities of nuclear weapons would enable us to reach out to new alternatives for caging the nuclear genie, even if we cannot return it to the bottle. And, finally, a well-informed public is perhaps even more important to calibrating our preparations for the possibility of chemical and biological warfare. Citizens could easily overreact to these odious threats. They need to understand that those threats are real but not inevitably catastrophic, especially if there is wide citizen participation in preventive and postattack defensive measures.

The world is at a turning point. The prospects for bringing nuclear weapons under international control are good, but if the United States does not provide firm, imaginative leadership, such weapons could proliferate dangerously instead. Chemical and biological weapons have rarely been used yet are threatening ominously. Again, it will take leadership from the United States to induce the world community to cage these genies at least as well as it has in the past.

The opportunity for global management of weapons of mass destruction is there. An informed public must demand that our government seize it in concert with as many other responsible nations as possible.

APPENDIX A:
LETHALITY OF NUCLEAR WEAPONS

The executive branch of our government has been negligent, even irresponsible, in underestimating the impact nuclear weapons would have. A good example of this is data derived by the Department of Defense and presented to Congress in March 1974 by Secretary of Defense James R. Schlesinger. In discussing the fatalities we might sustain in a Soviet attack against our nuclear forces, Schlesinger stated, "I am talking here about casualties of 15,000, 20,000, 25,000."[1] Six months later, Schlesinger revised that figure to the order of 1.5 million.[2] In another ten months, the Department of Defense, in a written response to Congress, revised the estimate upward to 3.2 million to 16.3 million. A survey conducted by the Congress's Office of Technology Assessment (OTA) found that an attack similar in dimension would most likely result in the deaths of 14 million people. Independent analysis using more sophisticated damage estimation models has resulted in significantly greater casualty estimates. One done by Princeton University's Center for Energy and Environmental Studies concluded that 7 million to 25 million people would die. This variation in estimated fatalities from 15,000 to 25 million is typical of the indifferent way in which the government has approached this subject.

Indifference is abetted by the shorthand terminology employed when dealing with the quantities of power involved in nuclear weaponry. It is simply difficult to write about a "one billion, one hundred million pound bomb," or to use endless zeros (e.g., "a 1,100,000,000 pound bomb"). Yet those are the only ways to describe a nuclear weapon that permit a fair comparison with the norm we hold—conventional bombs that range from 500 to 2,000 pounds. For convenience, we talk in terms of megatons (MT, millions of tons) or kilotons (KT, thousands of tons).

If START II is implemented, the standard intercontinental warhead in the Russian inventory will be 550 KT, that is, 550 × 1,000 (kilo) × 2,200 (lbs./metric tonne), or 1,210,000,000 pounds. It would take more than 25,000 sorties by our most modern bomber, the B-2, to deliver that much explosive in conventional munitions. It would take a freight train 150 miles long to transport it to the airfield.[3] Another comparison is that in the course of some 44,000 aircraft sorties during the six-week air campaign in the Gulf War with Iraq in 1991, we dropped about 84,000 tonnes of conventional bombs,[4] or less than one-fifth of the explosive equivalent of a single 550-KT nuclear bomb.

But there is a particular danger in this terminology: It becomes not so incongruous to talk about "small" nuclear warheads. When we label them as being "only" .1 KT, a warhead that would fit on an artillery shell, it sounds small. But .1 KT is the equivalent of .1 × 1,000 (kilo) × 2,200 (lbs./tonne), or 220,000 pounds of conventional explosive. One of the smallest warheads we have had in our inventory was a .1-KT artillery shell, but the power of one such shell was the equivalent, in conventional explosives, of five fully loaded B-2 bombers. Another perspective: "Three 1-MT nuclear explosions would release the same amount of energy as all bombs dropped in the six years of World War II."[5]

The danger of terminology leading to our misunderstanding lethality is compounded by the fact that these comparisons of tonnages consider only blast effects, which are all there is when talking about conventional munitions. But blast effects are only the beginning when talking about nuclear weapons. The additional effects of nuclear weapons are thermal energy, radioactivity, electromagnetic pulse, economic and societal disruption, and environmental damage. These can greatly increase the total effect.

It is in the area of these effects unique to nuclear weapons that the Executive Branch has not been sufficiently persevering. There are different reasons for each instance of underestimating or ignoring these effects.

Blast Effect

The detonation of a nuclear weapon creates a ball of superheated air that initially expands outward at millions of miles per hour. This expanding "fireball" acts like a fast-moving piston on the surrounding air, creating a shell of compressed air—the "shockwave"—of enormous power and extent. The shockwave propagates outward by pressing against the next layer of air, crushing that layer into a shell of air that in turn presses against the air layer beyond. This process leads not only to the forward motion of the shell of high-pressure air but also to high winds due to the inevitable flow of air from each successive layer to the next.

The shockwave can be thought of as having an "overpressure" or "static overpressure" that can crush objects in its path, and a "dynamic overpressure" due to the accompanying high winds that can knock down and tear apart structures. In general, large, well-constructed buildings are destroyed by the hammerlike effect of the arriving shockwave and the crushing effect of overpressure as the shock envelops the structure. In contrast, objects like trees and utility poles are not always susceptible to damage from the crushing effects of the pressure wave but are, instead, destroyed by the high winds that accompany the shock.[6]

As a shockwave passes over a target area it carries heavy objects lifted by the accompanying winds, and it will cause the damage or collapse of structures from the combined effects of high winds, the smashing effects of objects being carried by the winds, and the hammering and crushing effects of overpressure. Individuals may be killed, injured, or trapped as the structures around them collapse; if they are caught in the open they might be hit by wind-carried objects or be picked up and carried by the wind and thrown up against walls and the like. The pressure wave can thereby cause many deaths and injuries by numerous mechanisms that will depend on the luck or luckless circumstance of each victim in its path.

As an illustration, a shockwave from a nuclear explosion that generates five pounds per square inch (psi) static overpressure will be accompanied by winds of 160 miles per hour (mph). At Hiroshima and Nagasaki, the 5 psi range was a "lethal zone" for humans within which 50 percent were killed and some 30 percent more injured. At the 5 psi range, unreinforced brick and lesser buildings were destroyed; 200 to 600 bits per square yard of debris and shards of glass were sent flying about with lethal effect. A modern 550-KT nuclear bomb would generate such winds and a static overpressure of 5 psi out to 3.5 miles if the burst were in the air (that is, if the detonation were high enough that the fireball did not touch the ground).

If burst in contact with the ground, a 550-KT weapon would generate 5 psi out to only 2.3 miles; to a range of about 1.1 miles from ground zero the overpressure would be 20 psi and the winds more than 500 mph—sufficient to destroy many reinforced concrete structures. A groundburst weapon will maximize damage at ground zero and create extensive radiation effects, whereas an airburst will maximize the area affected by blast damage.

The executive branch employs a straightforward "cookie cutter" model to calculate overpressures for various nuclear detonations at various ranges from ground zero. It then scales the known casualty rates for those overpressures at Hiroshima to the population and nature of the area under consideration.

One way to place these data in perspective is to recognize that in terms of blast today's 550-KT weapon has forty times the yield of the one employed at Hiroshima.* Although scaling up by this much has its risks, the executive branch's estimates of blast effect seem reasonable.

Executive branch estimates do, however, ignore one effect of blast: "blast disruption fires." These fires may be started by ruptured natural gas lines, overturned electrical equipment with resulting short circuits, and other disrupted flammable facilities such as stoves, furnaces, and gasoline pumps. Here, the extent of fires would be dependent on the particular locale. Although blast disruption fires potentially could substantially enhance the damage from a nuclear explosion, many more fires will on average be set by the intense light flash from the fireball, discussed next.

Thermal Energy

The fireball created by a nuclear explosion will be much hotter than the surface of the sun for fractions of a second and will radiate light and heat, as do all objects of very high temperature. Because the fireball is so hot and close to the earth, it will deliver enormous amounts of heat and light to the terrain surrounding the detonation point, and it will be hundreds or thousands of times brighter than the sun at noon. If the fireball is created by the detonation of a 1-MT nuclear weapon, for example, within roughly eight- to nine-tenths of a second each section of its surface will be radiating about three times as much heat and light as a comparable area of the sun itself. The intense flash of light and heat from the explosion of a 550-KT weapon can carbonize exposed skin and cause clothing to ignite. At a range of three miles, for instance, surfaces would fulminate and recoil as they emanate flames, and even particles of sand would explode like pieces of popcorn from the rapid heating of the fireball. At three and a half miles, where the blast pressure would be about 5 psi, the fireball could ignite clothing on people, curtains and upholstery in homes and offices, and rubber tires on cars. At four miles, it could blister aluminum surfaces, and

---

*A yield 40 times greater does not result in 40 times as much destruction. A 1-MT weapon has 1,000 times the destructive yield of a 1-KT weapon, but the blast effects cover only 100 times as much area, although the thermal and radiation effects would be approximately 600–900 times as great.

at six to seven miles it could still set fire to dry leaves and grass. This flash of incredibly intense, nuclear-driven sunlight could simultaneously set an uncountable number of fires over an area of close to 100 square miles.

In executive branch estimates the range of lethal thermal effect is calculated by using the same scaling factor as with blast effect. This method, however, disregards the fact that the range of thermal effects scales up faster with increased weapon yield than do blast effects. Thus, weapons larger than that employed at Hiroshima will set fires and burn people at greater distances than the blast effect will kill them.

The lethality of thermal effects depends on weather (clear or murky), but uncertainties due to weather variations, surprisingly, are not larger than the uncertainties in blast effects. Simply speaking, the variations in blast effects tend to be deemphasized and ignored, yet the government argues that variations in thermal effects make them difficult to predict.

Another serious thermal effect on urban areas is the firestorm that will follow. This firestorm results from the many fires initiated by the intense light and heat thrown off by the fireball. Executive branch estimates of casualties from nuclear attacks ignore this lethal consequence of nuclear attack: "Due to the large area of the fire, the fire zone would act as a gigantic air pump, driving enormous volumes of air skyward. As cooler air is drawn in to replace the air pumped away, the pumping action would create very high ground winds. Large amounts of poisonous smoke and gases would be generated and could therefore kill many more people than blast effects alone."[7] During World War II, firestorms resulting from incendiary bombings devastated Tokyo and Dresden; firestorms consumed Hiroshima and Nagasaki as a result of nuclear attacks.

"Conflagration" models developed to estimate damage and deaths from all kinds of fires conclude there will be 1.5–4.1 times more deaths than the executive branch estimates. These results have been rejected on the grounds that in any particular circumstance they are dependent on the amount of moisture in combustible materials in the area, the local weather and atmospheric visibility, and other factors that will influence the likelihood of fire ignitions (snow cover during winter or large amounts of dry underbrush during summer). These may well be cause to accept the low end of the 1.5–4.1 prediction as minimal for planning purposes—but not to ignore the consideration. One specific study that postulated 100 1-MT attacks on U.S. cities estimated that using blast effects only, there would be about 14 million fatalities; employing conflagration models would increase that to 23–56 million, depending on the assumptions.[8]

Finally, executive branch estimates of thermal casualties are low because many of the survivors with burns would die for lack of medical treatment. There are, for instance, specialized facilities for treating only about 2,000 burn victims in the entire country.[9] Moreover, people with burns might also have received high doses of radiation. Radiation exposure would depress their immune systems and greatly increase the probability of death from the complications of both burns and damage to immune systems.

Radioactivity

When matter is converted into energy, by either fission or fusion, one result is gamma radiation that is delivered in the form of electromagnetic waves similar to light and X-rays but with greater ability to penetrate materials. Another type of harmful radiation that is generated by nuclear explosives is neutron radiation, which is delivered as a "particle of unit mass."* These radioactive emissions have both prompt and delayed effects on people and the environment.

Prompt radiation from either an airburst or groundburst consists of gamma rays and neutrons emitted within the first minute. In high concentrations they can endanger humans. The general rule is that this radioactivity would be immediately fatal to humans only out to about where the individuals would die anyway from blast or thermal effects, although this is not true for weapons below 20 KT.[10] Executive branch estimates of deaths do take prompt radiation into account.

Delayed radiation, often called "fallout," occurs when a nuclear explosion takes place on the ground or at low altitude. Since the explosion derives its energy from nuclear reactions, large amounts of radioactive materials are created as a by-product of these reactions. When a detonation occurs at or near the ground, these radioactive materials get sucked into the rising fireball and become mixed with other debris. The rising fireball eventually carries these radioactive materials into the upper atmosphere, from where they are then deposited back minutes, hours, or days after the explosion. The groundburst of a 550-KT weapon can create a contaminated crater 800 feet in diameter and 165 feet deep. In so doing, hundreds of thousands of tons of dirt are lifted along with the radioactive materials from the bomb and thrust together upward. The heavier pieces of dirt carrying radioactive materials will fall back to earth within hours or days, creating a radiation hazard at significant distances from ground zero. For instance, a 500-KT groundburst could deliver enough radiation sixty to seventy miles downwind to kill all unprotected people within days if they did not take shelter or evacuate the area. Thirty miles downwind the outcome could be the same within four to five hours of the explosion.

A related example is the nonnuclear explosion, fire, and radioactive release in the nuclear power plant at Chernobyl in 1986. As a result of this accident, 1,200 square miles adjacent to the reactor were so contaminated that humans are still excluded; some 30,000 square miles of farmland can be only partially cultivated. The lighter radioactive particles can be carried on the winds as they decay or eventually be deposited back on earth as radioactive fallout over weeks or months and at distances of thousands of miles. For example, Chernobyl delivered mild contamination from fallout as far as northern Norway, some 1,500 miles distant.

There are many structures in Russia and the United States that have some level of blast resistance. In order to account for the higher blast resistance of these structures, we can detonate nuclear weapons at lower altitudes. For example, if an airfield contained aircraft shelters that were able to resist a 100-psi blast (aircraft shelters are usually considerably harder than this) a 550-KT weapon would have to be detonated at an altitude of less than a half-mile in order to maximize damage. Under these conditions, even though the detonation is not a surface burst, considerable fallout could be expected. This illustrates why it is likely that in a nuclear war with thousands of nuclear detonations, in all likelihood most such detonations would cause heavy fallout.

---

*L. W. McNaught, *Nuclear Weapons and Their Effects* (London: Brassey's Defence Publishers, 1984), p. 50. Two other forms of radiation are present during a nuclear explosion. These are alpha radiation, which can be stopped by a single sheet of paper, and beta radiation, which also has little penetrating power. These two forms of radiation are generally considered insignificant to the overall calculation of lethal effects in the event of a nuclear explosion.

There are models to estimate both the effects of fallout on people and the size of any area near ground zero that will be contaminated. These models are built around the time of year, the prevailing weather patterns, and the type of protective measures individuals will take. In utilizing such models, the executive branch tends to assume an unrealistic degree of protection for the individual, for example, warning time to seek shelter; civil defense shelters, basements, or brick residences; whether people are willing to remain sheltered for weeks or even months; and whether supplies of food, water, and hygienic facilities have been prestocked. Perhaps the strongest reason to question whether the populace can be as protected as the government estimates is that the average citizen does not know how to seek protection. Civil defense has never caught on in our country. Thus, the thesis that survival would be greatly enhanced if people could keep several feet of dirt between them and any residual radioactivity for several weeks is less than useful.[11] The odds of getting massive numbers of Americans to understand civil defense and to practice it are nil.

The standard used in government estimates for human tolerance to radiation may also be overly optimistic, according to research on animals as well as data on residents of the Marshall Islands, who were accidentally irradiated in the test of a nuclear weapon.[12]

Further, government estimates are low because they are limited to fatalities that occur within the first thirty days following an attack. There clearly will be more deaths after that, and even during those first thirty days people with radiation sickness will be a drain on the process of recovery.

Another facet of radiation is the amount of land that would be contaminated by groundbursts or low-altitude bursts, to the point it could not be inhabited for a considerable period of time. This could be in and around the crater at ground zero; it could also result from the immediate fallout in the nearby area or from later, more distant fallout. A 1-MT groundburst would, for instance, "result in the removal from cultivation of the equivalent of one million acres for seven years if the contaminated land were cultivated before the nuclear event."[13] The effect of being denied access to such sizable areas is not considered at all in executive branch estimates, largely because the amount and location of fallout are subject to many variables such as wind and weather. There is also no consideration of the fact that current and future food supplies would be at risk if the contaminated areas happened to be farmland. That, in turn, could raise psychological problems as people worried whether the food they were receiving was safe to eat.

Electromagnetic Pulse

EMP is an intense electric and magnetic pulse that is created by the gamma radiation that emanates from a nuclear detonation. The large electric fields created in this way produce high-voltage and current pulses in the electric circuits they encounter. These electric fields build to peak voltages many times faster than a lightning bolt, thereby overwhelming most devices that have been designed to protect electrical and electronic devices from surges in current and voltage. EMP from even a groundburst could knock out power grids, electrical equipment, and telephones as well as destroy computer memories six to twelve miles from ground zero (although not all such equipment would necessarily be damaged as the coupling of EMP is very dependent on many details of the circuits and not readily predictable). A burst at an altitude of 200 miles over Nebraska designed to produce EMP could shut down the national power grid, destroy computer memories, and knock out unprotected communications systems across the country.[14] EMP would affect the immediate ability of governmental authorities to manage the society, and repairing the damage would consume a considerable effort in the early reconstruction period. It is another area of neglect in executive branch estimates.

Environmental Effect

Since trees and many other plants are roughly as susceptible to radiation exposure as are people, any area exposed to levels of radiation high enough to kill or injure people would be deforested or depleted of plant life. This, in turn, would have implications for soil erosion and for the survival prospects of wild and domesticated animals (assuming that direct radiation exposure did not kill them outright). The sudden killing or stressing of some species by radiation could have unforeseen effects on the environmental balance. For example, insects, which are more resistant to radiation than birds, would no longer be subject to predation. This, in turn, could lead to wild fluctuations in the size of insect populations in the new ecological system created by the elimination of important predators and plant life.

Multiple nuclear explosions could also create sufficient nitric oxides to deplete the ozone layer twenty to thirty kilometers above the earth. This would expose humans and animals to higher-than-normal ultraviolet radiation. Although the physics of ozone depletion is not fully understood and cannot be quantified, the consequences of ozone depletion could be serious. There is also the thesis of "nuclear winter," in which vast fires started by an extensive nuclear attack would send sufficient smoke and particles into the atmosphere to cut off the sun for an extended period, with a subsequent cooling effect. Although the surface temperature might not change as severely as suggested by early predictions of nuclear winter, there are enough effects associated with this phenomenon that nuclear winter cannot be discounted entirely.

Economic and Social Disruption

The most serious area of underestimation by the executive branch is the disruptive effects on the economy and the society. It is the area that is most difficult to quantify. The effects of blast, thermal energy, fires, and radiation are measured by the number of fatalities and injured; the number of hardened structures, such as reinforced buildings or missile silos, destroyed; and the size of the area of soft structures leveled. Disruption of the economy and the society is measured by the interruption of services and supplies. These impact on far more than the area that has been attacked. Some examples with respect to the economy:

- If Chicago's railroad marshaling yards were destroyed, commerce moving across the country would be severely affected. Just how much would be determined by whether alternate routes, such as through St. Louis, have also been attacked.
- Much the same would be the case with one or several attacks on major airports. Our economy is highly dependent on rapid transportation, and there is little excess airport capacity.
- The disruption of Wall Street would bring the country's financial apparatus to a halt. Records of credit card and banking transactions and ownership of securities and properties could be destroyed.

- Attacks on our ICBM silos in the farm belt would contaminate farmland and crops. This, combined with disruptions in the food distribution network, could result in areas of starvation. Loss of agricultural productivity would also imperil our principal source of foreign exchange.
- Attacks on only a few harbors, refineries, and pipelines could deny the supply of crude oil into and throughout the country, resulting in crippling shortages of fuel for heating, automobiles, trucks, railroads, and industry.
- The interruption of supply chains due to fuel shortages, transportation bottlenecks, and the destruction of factories would ripple throughout our economy, which is finely tuned to "just in time" deliveries.
- The interruption of message communication links, computer networks, and electrical power grids by EMP would play havoc with economic activity across the board and with the government's effort of recovery.

There would also be equally serious problems in maintaining social cohesion:

- Federal, state, and local governments could have difficulty establishing sufficient communications to maintain order and direct the recovery effort.
- The contamination from even one bomb could displace hundreds of thousands of people and possibly lead to panic in evacuations—even looting and a general breakdown of law and order.
- With the death of perhaps half a million people over a period of just a few weeks in a single city from a single 1-MT nuclear blast, the loss of loved ones and the task of their burial would be psychologically traumatic. Moreover, it would seem never ending as radiation sickness gradually took its toll.
- Contamination of food supplies in rumor or fact could test civility and order.
- Fires could range on a scale that few fire departments could handle under normal conditions. In many cases, fire departments themselves would be destroyed, being without access to water supplies or simply unable to move through the rubble to where they are needed.
- Medical services could be stretched to the point that severe triage would be necessary. By government estimate, even if only one city were attacked by a single nuclear weapon, the remaining medical resources for the rest of the entire country would be inadequate to care for the half-million or so injured in that city, over and above those killed. And interruptions in water, electrical, and sanitation services could make the medical problem even worse and raise the specter of epidemics.

At some point, the overall psychological impact could be so great that society might not have the will to pull itself back together or, even if it did, the capability to do so. If the attacks are on only one or two cities, that is not likely to be the case. The Japanese reconstructed Hiroshima and Nagasaki reasonably quickly, and these have become relatively normal cities once again. The issue of ultimate recovery arises if there are more than only a few nuclear attacks, because damage to the society as a whole from two detonations would not be the sum of the two individual damages—but something greater. For instance, recovery at Hiroshima and Nagasaki was highly dependent on outside resources coming to the rescue. If many of the cities that helped Hiroshima and Nagasaki had also been attacked they too would have been seeking aid, not supplying it. At some number of detonations, sufficient sources of outside support would no longer be available to some areas. Each additional detonation would cut off more sources, until enough areas were hopelessly adrift that the society would fracture into regional societies and cease to function as a political and economic entity.

Overall Effect

There is no mathematical way to add up the effects of underestimation in all of the various areas mentioned above, and the total distortion would vary with the specific circumstances. My subjective evaluation, however, is that our government underestimates by a factor between two and eight.

TABLE A.1   Effects of Conventional and Nuclear Weapons

Effect	Conventional	Nuclear
Blast	✓	✓
Thermal Energy		✓
Radioactivity		✓
Electromagnetic Pulse		✓
Economic and Social Disruption		✓
Environmental Damage		✓

TABLE A.2   Summary of Executive Branch Estimating of the Effects of Nuclear Detonations

Effect	Estimated Satisfactorily	Under-estimated	Ignored
Blast			
Damage to property and people	✓		
Fires ignited by blast effects			✓
Thermal			
Direct ignition and burns fatal to people		✓	
Firestorms			✓
Radioactivity			
Prompt fatalities	✓		
Delayed fatalities from fallout			
Within 30 days		✓	
After 30 days			✓
Irradiation of ground areas			✓
Electromagnetic Pulse			
Disruption of electricity and communications			✓
Economic and Social Disruption			✓
Environmental Damage			
Depletion of plant life			✓
Ozone depletion			✓
Nuclear winter			✓

TABLE A.3   Blast Effects of a 550-KT Explosion 5,000 Feet Above the Earth

Distance from Ground Zero (miles)	Peak Overpressure (above atmosphere)	Peak Wind (mph)	Typical Effects
1.4	20 psi	507	Reinforced concrete structures leveled
2.2	10 psi	296	Most factories and commercial buildings collapse
3.3	5 psi	164	Lightly constructed commercial buildings destroyed; heavier construction severely damaged; houses collapse
4.5	3 psi	102	Walls of steel-frame buildings blown away; severe damage to residences; winds kill people in the open
8.7	1 psi	36	Damage to structures; people endangered by flying glass and debris

SOURCE: Adapted from U.S. Congress, Office of Technology Assessment, *The Effects of Nuclear War* (Washington, D.C.: Government Printing Office, 1990), p. 18.

APPENDIX B:
EXCERPTS FROM "NUCLEAR CRASH—THE U.S. ECONOMY AFTER SMALL NUCLEAR ATTACKS"

M. Anjali Sastry, Joseph J. Romm, Kosta Tsipis

The effects of a nuclear attack on a country's society and economy have been the subject of numerous studies based on data from the nuclear bombs used against Hiroshima and Nagasaki, from nuclear tests, and from conventional-bomb damage data.[1] Even though these studies have focused on quantitative calculations of the physical damage and have presented only qualitative extrapolations of the effects of this damage on the fate of the survivors, they were instrumental in establishing the fact that a nuclear exchange between two warring nations would result in tremendous devastation.

Studies done under government contract in the U.S. have until very recently shown that the U.S. economy can survive a limited nuclear attack. For example, a 1973 report by SRI on an input-output computer model simulation of the economy predicted complete economic recovery from a nuclear attack within a decade and a half—*regardless* of the attack size, which varied from 4% to 20% of the Soviet arsenal.

But very different results are reached by a 1980 systems dynamics computer model simulation of the post-attack U.S. economy that was commissioned by the Federal Emergency Management Agency (FEMA). The new FEMA model predicts the collapse of the U.S. economy following an attack much smaller than those SRI studied. To rebuild the economy to anything near its previous levels would take many decades.

If different models lead to different conclusions, how can one decide which one is best approximating the grim post-attack reality. We will examine both the SRI and FEMA models and show how the former was *bound* to give misleading results, while the latter was specifically designed to minimize or avoid many problems inherent in previous computer models of the post-attack economy.

Previous models were designed to operate within historical bounds, with the economy in equilibrium, and so were unrealistic in their representation of the post-attack economy, which could very well be out of equilibrium for extended periods of time. Previous models have tended to be simple, linear, growth models that reproduce the historical behavior of the U.S. economy—sustained growth—almost immediately after much larger attacks than we consider here. The FEMA model, on the other hand, is designed to handle both equilibrium and non-equilibrium conditions. It is composed of hundreds of non-linear, recursive equations. And, while these equations reflect the historical performance of the economy, they are also designed to reflect specific actions taken by economic decisionmakers (consumers, government officials, and corporate executives). Therefore, while the FEMA model can reproduce historical patterns, it is not "forced" to.

The technique the FEMA model uses, Systems Dynamics, is more interactive, more dynamic, and more flexible than methods previously used for simulations of the post-attack economy. In addition, we have based our analyses on: 1) the latest, most realistic estimates of the effects of nuclear weapons, 2) a detailed study of the distribution of key U.S. industries, and 3) an extensive Census Bureau database of U.S. population and manufacturing capacity. Nevertheless, the FEMA model is only a computer model, and while it may be more rigorous than the "mental" models we all use to anticipate the behavior of the world, its results should be viewed cautiously. For instance, the FEMA model is not capable of predicting precise quantitative results, such as the exact level of GNP 20 years after an attack. The results it most reliably produces are qualitative trends, such as the inability of the GNP to recover for decades.

It deserves mention that the computer model used here is not exactly the same as that used in the FEMA report approved for public release in November 1980. Over the last several years, some of the original authors, as well as our group, have worked to fix some of the errors in that program, and have improved its ability to model the U.S. economy.

This report presents the preliminary results of a study that explores the predictive capability of the FEMA simulation program and the degree to which computer modeling can provide reliable predictions of the behavior of the U.S. economy after a nuclear attack. The study was undertaken with several purposes in mind:

A. To determine whether the discrepancy between older static simulation models and the FEMA model is significant in the context of decisions about the nuclear policy of the country.
B. To determine the minimum number of nuclear explosives that would create a perturbation severe enough to collapse the U.S. economy; that is, the number that would be an unquestionable deterrent in the hands of the Soviets. This number, augmented to allow for certainty of delivery, could then become a guideline for future nuclear arms limitation negotiations. For instance, both sides could reduce to a number that would assure them of the ability to deliver the nuclear explosives that would collapse the other side's economy. (FEMA has commissioned a similar computer simulation of the Soviet economy.)
C. To provide a measurement for the efficiency required of a strategic defensive shield designed to permit the U.S. economy to survive a full Soviet nuclear attack.

We have used the FEMA program that simulates the U.S. economy to examine the results of small nuclear attacks that would collapse the U.S. economy. We were looking for the most effective "bottleneck" mechanisms for collapse, and as a consequence we have focused particular attention on liquid fossil fuels. Transportation, energy production, and many crucial industry products depend on liquid fuels. We have found that the shock of denying these resources to the U.S. for even a relatively short period of time disintegrates the economy. This rapid economic deterioration—the "nuclear crash"—could mean that within months of an attack most of the population would starve to death and that the survivors would be reduced to near-medieval levels of existence for decades.

We find that these predictions are not particularly sensitive to the destructiveness assumed for individual attacking weapons. We demonstrate that even using consistently conservative assumptions—which lead to overestimates of the likelihood of a U.S. national economic recovery—an attack consisting of as little as *1% or 2% of the Soviet nuclear arsenal* could cause a complete and long-lasting economic crash in the United States.

At every turn of the research our assumptions, introduced into the computer program either explicitly—as initial values of variables—or implicitly, have been uniformly conservative. We have tested the sensitivity of the computer model over a large range of assumptions, and we present the results of simulation in only those cases when we have biased the assumptions towards recovery of the economy. Yet the perturbations caused by the small, bottlenecking attack scenarios we tested consistently demonstrate the vulnerability of the U.S. economy to a Soviet attack that would not exceed 1% to 2% of their nuclear arsenal.

It bears repeating that the FEMA program we used cannot simulate with high analytical precision the effects of the selective destruction of very small though crucial sectors of the U.S. economy—destruction which we believe would drastically affect the economy. Moreover, limitations exist in any computer model of the economy . . . , and so our results must be read as suggestive rather than definitive. Real nuclear attacks would doubtless be much worse than the FEMA model indicates.

This appendix consists of . . . the most recent information regarding the effects of nuclear explosives on civilian targets. Consistent with our conservative approach we have incorporated into the simulation only two destructive effects, blast and heat, ignoring the effects of the nuclear electromagnetic pulse (EMP) and of delayed radioactive fallout on the U.S. economy. We believe that EMP would in fact have devastating effects on communications and other electronic equipment, including computers, and that fallout would drastically limit the use of undamaged industrial-production capacity and food-producing farm lands, and consequently their inclusion would exacerbate economic dysfunction. But we could not incorporate these effects into the simulation program in a way that would lead to reliable predictions of their impact on the evolution of the economy after the attack.

Then, we consider the effects of three different attack scenarios on the U.S. economy. The first is an attack which destroys 60% of the population and 40% of the industry, which we call the 60/40 Attack. The smallest of the three attacks, the Counter-Energy Attack, destroys only commercial ports and the refining and storage facilities for liquid fossil fuels. The third attack destroys, in addition to the fuel facilities, some key manufacturing sectors such as electronics, primary metals production, and heavy machines. This we call the Counter-Energy Counter-Industry Attack. We present the results in the form of graphs (see Figures B.1 through B.9), with some discussion.

Because of the very large number of assumptions we have necessarily made in exploring the effects of these attacks, two things must be borne firmly in mind when reading this report. First, that the results are uniformly *optimistic*, erring towards the best-case view at every point of choice, and second, that it is *trends* rather than absolute values that one should focus on in reading the report.

Results

In this [section] we will examine the predictions the FEMA model makes for the three baseline attack scenarios: the 60/40 attack (which corresponds to the standard counter-population and counter-industry scenario), the counter-energy attack, and the counter-energy attack augmented with a counter-industry component targeted at key economic sectors like primary metals manufacturing. To test the robustness of the results, we consider a variety of inputs to each of these scenarios.

The Counter-Energy Attack

The counter-energy attack consists of 85 550-kiloton weapons and 154 200-kiloton weapons, a total of 239 nuclear weapons that add up to 110 equivalent megatons—under 2% of the deployed equivalent megatonnage of the Soviet Union. In absolute megatons the attack is even smaller, under 1% of the total Soviet megatons.

The attack is designed to inflict the maximum economic damage while minimizing the attack size; to do this, only the facilities that refine, store and transport liquid fuels are targeted. Although urban areas are not deliberately targeted in this scenario, most of the major U.S. cities end up receiving one or more weapons. This is a by-product of the targeting strategy, which blasts every commercial dock and berth capable of bringing imports into the nation with at least 5 psi.[2] Other explicitly targeted facilities include the nation's Strategic Petroleum Reserve, maintained at five Texas and Louisiana sites by the Department of Energy as a protection against a sudden drop of liquid-fuel availability.[3] Over 95% of all operating U.S. refineries[4] are destroyed by this attack, which also obliterates almost every inactive refinery. The attack targets the major nodes—junctions of over five lines, terminals, and pump or compressor stations—of the nation's three pipeline systems, which are used to transport crude petroleum, petroleum products, and natural gas.[5] Although industrial installations are not selected as targets, the attack also destroys 25% of the nation's primary steel manufacturing capacity and 18% of primary nonferrous-metals manufacturing (many

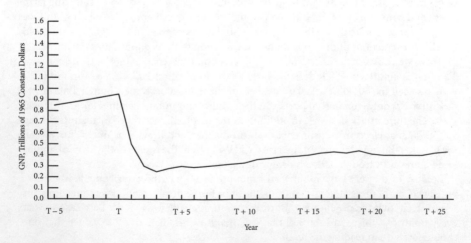

FIGURE B.1   Counter-energy attack: baseline conditions

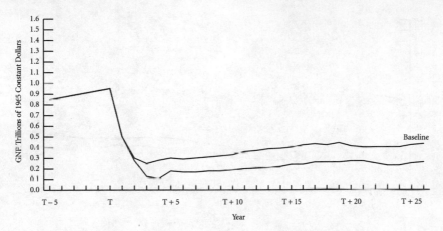

FIGURE B.2   Counter-energy attack: mild psychological effects

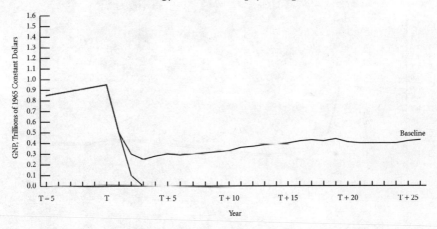

FIGURE B.3   Counter-energy attack: moderate psychological effects

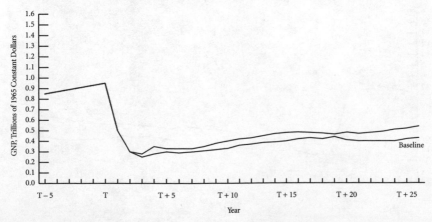

FIGURE B.4   Counter-energy attack: food imports doubled

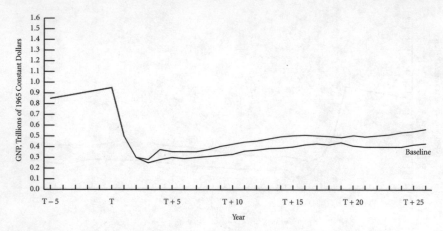

FIGURE B.5   Counter-energy attack: all imports doubled

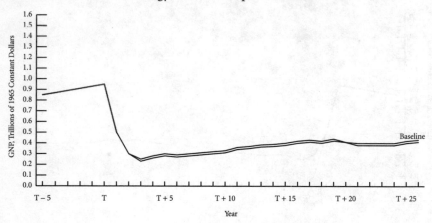

FIGURE B.6   Counter-energy attack: all imports reduced

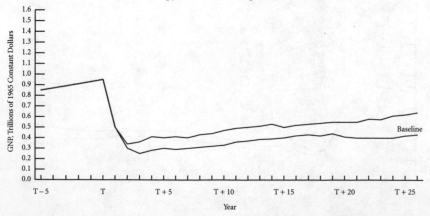

FIGURE B.7   Counter-energy attack: faster rate of transportation reconnection

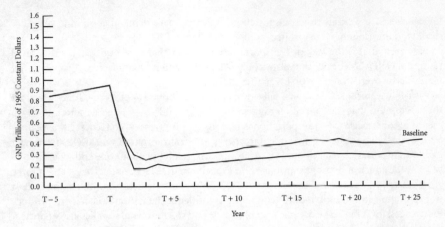

FIGURE B.8   Counter-energy attack: slower rate of transportation reconnection

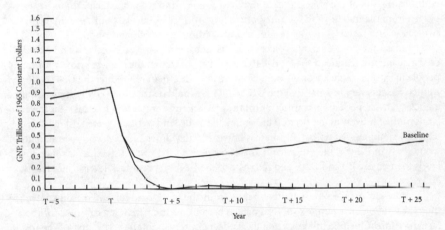

FIGURE B.9   Counter-energy attack: slower rate of transportation reconnection with mild psychological effects

metals-producing plants tend to be located near port and refinery facilities). In all, the U.S. loses 33% of its capacity to produce energy products, 19% of its capacity to make metals, and between 5% and 10% of its capacity to manufacture other products; overall, the U.S. economy loses 8% of its manufacturing capacity. About twenty million Americans die immediately following this attack, which also injures five million; casualties total 10%.

Despite our consistent use of conservative assumptions to estimate damage and casualty rates, the model simulations indicate that the consequences of the counter-energy attack would be severe (see figures in this appendix, where we present a representative set of the graphical output and a discussion of its interpretation). In a scenario that optimistically allows 10% of the pre-attack rate of energy imports and 20% of the pre-attack rate of all other imports to arrive in the U.S. immediately after the attack (with much higher levels in subsequent years— for instance, energy imports double in about one year), includes no psychological effects, and posits that transportation capacity equals demand about one year after the attack, the economy is devastated, as plotted in Figure B.1.

As expected, it is the lack of transportation adequacy that is responsible for the initial plunge in GNP. . . . The attack destroys only 8% of the nation's manufacturing capacity, but GNP falls by over 50% in the first year after the attack.

Available transportation capital falls immediately to about 5% of its pre-attack level. Yet the assumption that transportation capacity equals demand about one year after the attack means in some sense that transportation is no longer a "bottleneck" to recovery one year after the attack. The policy of investment in energy and transportation we have assumed here brings transportation capacity to 50% of its pre-attack level in about one and a half to two years of the attack and brings transportation capacity to near its pre-attack level about three years after the attack. Yet even with these exceedingly optimistic assumptions, the lack of transportation in the early months continues to influence the nation's capacity to produce for decades; for if in these early years people starve and stocks of vital supplies are exhausted, it can take many, many years to undo the harmful effects.

About 8% of the population is killed directly by weapons effects, but almost 60% die within two years of the attack. People starve to death without food, which cannot be transported from the middle of the country where it is produced to the large urban centers on the two coasts, and factories cannot produce goods without materials and labor.

The mass starvation that takes place after this attack (and other attacks) should be considered a qualitative feature of the model. It seems likely to us that the highest priority for many people in the post-attack world would be survival, rather than rebuilding the U.S. economy. In this case, it is very possible that the U.S. economy would be transformed dramatically after a nuclear attack, perhaps becoming far more agrarian; mass migration to areas near the crop lands of the Midwest might occur. This would allow the land to be cultivated using labor-intensive techniques that do not rely on fossil fuels and machinery. In this way, mass starvation would be avoided. On the other hand, if this occurred, GNP would stabilize at much lower levels than Figure B.1 indicates, and recovery of the GNP to pre-attack levels could take several decades.[6]

To represent people removing themselves from the workforce for any reason (to insure their survival or their family's survival or just because of the psychological shock of the attack), we might include mild psychological effects in the counter-energy attack. The result, indicated in Figure B.2, shows the economy languishing at about a quarter of its pre-attack level for 20 years. It bears repeating that mild psychological effects are rather mild: If the GNP is falling at a rate of 50% per year, the main effect on the economy is that worker productivity falls by a few percent.

Moderate psychological effects have an even more devastating effect on the economy, causing complete economic collapse within three years of the attack, as shown in Figure B.3.

Until the end of the discussion of the counter-energy attack, we will turn off the psychological effects sector of the FEMA model and consider that there is no adverse psychological reaction to the attack. This optimistic assumption will allow us to examine independently the effects of changing the values of other inputs to the model.

Although we consider the level of imports we allot for this attack to be optimistic, we also examine even higher levels of imports. First, we test the original import rates—10% fuel, 20% other goods—augmented by doubling the import availability of food to 40% in just the first year after the attack (as before, these levels are relative to the pre-attack import rates and they are incremented every subsequent year). The results are shown in Figure B.4. GNP is consistently about 15% higher. Fewer people starve, and the economy consequently can perform better. When all imports are doubled, to a rate of 20% for fuel and 40% for other goods, again with higher levels in subsequent years, GNP follows a similar path (see Figure B.5), indicating that it is the food imports that are important. Even higher rates of imports were tested, and while they tended to improve the economy somewhat in the short term, they were not so beneficial in the long term, insofar as they induced the economy to depend on imports, rather than rebuild its own manufacturing base. This is perhaps not surprising, in the light of the events of the past several years.[7]

The conditions represented in the two preceding test runs are probably unrealistically optimistic. Every commercial port that can be used to import significant quantities of goods and materials was destroyed in the counter energy attack scenario, after all, and every major city targeted. States that had in the past done a great deal of importing would be struggling just to save survivors. Moreover, it is far from clear that other countries will be in a position to help us, for they may be struggling in a global depression following the crash of the U.S. economy, or they may be directly targeted (as seems very possible in the case of Canada or Mexico).[8] At the very least, food imports will be very hard to come by after the U.S. stops exporting mass quantities and starts importing. More likely conditions would probably be import rates lower than our baseline rates, with energy imports initially reduced to a trickle, say, 5%. If we permit 15% of all other imports to be brought into the nation, we find that lowering import availability after the counter-energy attack reduces GNP performance only slightly, as shown in Figure B.6.

The transportation reconnection rate turns out to be an important determinant of the recovery rate. Although we consider our baseline conditions optimistic, we consider a policy which results in transportation capacity exceeding demand within months of the attack and has the vast majority of transportation capital returning within two years of the attack. As Figure B.7 shows, GNP is higher and recovery is faster, yet even in this very optimistic case, where the transportation bottleneck lasts less than a year, the economy is devastated and large instabilities threaten recovery.

In Figure B.8 we show the effect of a slower reconnection rate. Here, the prospects for any kind of recovery at all appear bleak. In this case, it takes two years for half of the transportation capital to be reintegrated, at about which time capacity exceeds demand and transportation is no longer a bottleneck to recovery. For many reasons, we believe these assumptions are far more realistic than our baseline conditions.

For instance, an extremely optimistic feature of the model is its assumption that scarce resources are allocated in ways that are optimal to recovery. After a real nuclear war, however, it seems much more likely that scarce resources would be allocated haphazardly (or that the military might simply appropriate them). Therefore, all of the results presented here are already biased towards predictions of recovery in situations that in reality could cause the immediate downward plunge of GNP characteristic of complete collapse. Yet our simulations that show GNP stagnating at levels a small fraction of pre-attack GNP cannot be considered recovery; indeed, one of the few things we can be fairly confident about in such cases is that the economy is not recovering.

As we have said, our baseline conditions combine several assumptions we believe to be optimistic. If we made just two of those assumptions more realistic—adding mild psychological effects to the slower recommendation rate for transportation—the counter-energy attack collapses the economy, as shown in Figure B.9. As before, transportation capacity exceeds demand within two years, yet by this time the population has dwindled and incentives to increase the recovery simply do not work: The survivors are discouraged. In the second post-attack decade, as the anticipated recovery fails to materialize, public confidence plunges further and workers begin to withdraw from the organized economy, possibly to take part in fractionalized, low-level forms of economic activity. It is this migration that finally causes the complete collapse of the U.S. economy.

This is perhaps the most realistic path for the economy after the counter-energy attack.

Source

Program in Science and Technology for International Security, M.I.T. 20A–001 Cambridge, MA 02139; Report #17, June 1987.

Appendix C:
Calculation of Russian Forces Surviving a U.S. Preemptive Attack

TABLE C.1   3,000 Russian Warheads

Number	Type Weapon	Percent Attrition	Number Surviving
300	Fixed ICBMs	90	30
300	Mobile ICBMs	50	150
800	SLBMs at sea	50	400
800	SLBMs in port	90	80
800	ALCMs on bombers	50	400
Total 3,000		Total surviving U.S. attack	1,060

Attrition of the surviving 1,060 Russian Warheads
while conducting retaliatory attacks on the United States

Type Attrition	Percent Attrition	Number Surviving
Friction		
180 ICBMs	10	162
480 SLBMs	10	432
400 ALCMs	10	360
Ballistic Missile Defense		
Versus 162 ICBMs	70	49
Versus 432 SLBMs	70	130
Other defenses versus 360 ALCMs	0	360
	Total penetrating to United States	539

Alternative calculation of attrition of 1,060 warheads during attack

Type Attrition	Percent Attrition	Number Surviving
Friction		
180 ICBMs	10	162
480 SLBMs	10	432
400 ALCMs	10	360
Ballistic Missile Defense		
Versus 162 ICBMs	90	16
Versus 432 SLBMs	90	43
Other defenses versus 360 ALCMs	0	360
	Total penetrating to United States	419

Second alternative calculation of attrition of 1,060 warheads during attack

Type Attrition	Percent Attrition	Number Surviving
Friction		
180 ICBMs	50	90
480 SLBMs	50	240
400 ALCMs	50	200
Ballistic Missile Defense		
Versus 90 ICBMs	90	9
Versus 240 SLBMs	90	24
Other defenses versus 200 ALCMs	0	200
	Total penetrating to United States	233

TABLE C.2   1,000 Russian Warheads (Same percentages by weapon type as Case 1)

Number	Type Weapon	Percent Attrition	Number Surviving
100	Fixed ICBMs	90	10
100	Mobile ICBMs	50	50
266	SLBMs at sea	50	133
266	SLBMs in port	90	27
268	ALCMs on bombers	50	134
Total 1,000		Total surviving U.S. attack	354

Attrition of the surviving 354 Russian Warheads
while conducting retaliatory attacks on the United States

Type Attrition	Percent Attrition	Number Surviving
Friction		
60 ICBMs	10	54
160 SLBMs	10	144
134 ALCMs	10	120
Ballistic Missile Defense		
Versus 54 ICBMs	70	16
Versus 144 SLBMs	70	43
Other defenses versus 120 ALCMs	0	120
	Total penetrating to United States	179

Alternative calculation of attrition of 354 warheads during attack

Type Attrition	Percent Attrition	Number Surviving
Friction		
60 ICBMs	10	54
160 SLBMs	10	144
134 ALCMs	10	120
Ballistic Missile Defense		
Versus 54 ICBMs	90	5
Versus 144 SLBMs	90	14
Other defenses versus 120 ALCMs	0	120
	Total penetrating to United States	139

Second alternative calculation of attrition of 354 warheads during attack

Type Attrition	Percent Attrition	Number Surviving
Friction		
60 ICBMs	50	30
160 SLBMs	50	80
134 ALCMs	50	67
Ballistic Missile Defense		
Versus 30 ICBMs	90	3
Versus 80 SLBMs	90	8
Other defenses versus 66 ALCMs	0	67
	Total Penetrating to United States	78

TABLE C.3   250 Russian Warheads (Same percentages by weapon type as Case 1)

Number	Type Weapon	Percent Attrition	Number Surviving
25	Fixed ICBMs	90	3
25	Mobile ICBMs	50	13
66	SLBMs at sea	50	33
66	SLBMs in port	90	7
68	ALCMs on bombers	50	34
Total 250		Total surviving U.S. attack	90

Attrition of the surviving 90 Russian Warheads
while conducting retaliatory attacks on the United States

Type Attrition	Percent Attrition	Number Surviving
Friction		
16 ICBMs	10	14
40 SLBMs	10	36
34 ALCMs	10	30
Ballistic Missile Defense		
Versus 14 ICBMs	70	4
Versus 36 SLBMs	70	11
Other defenses versus 30 ALCMs	0	30
	Total penetrating to United States	45

Alternative calculation of attrition of 90 warheads during attack

Type Attrition	Percent Attrition	Number Surviving
Friction		
16 ICBMs	10	14
40 SLBMs	10	36
34 ALCMs	10	30
Ballistic Missile Defense		
Versus 14 ICBMs	90	1
Versus 36 SLBMs	90	4
Other defenses versus 30 ALCMs	0	30
	Total penetrating to United States	35

(continues)

Second alternative calculation of attrition of 90 warheads during attack

Type Attrition	Percent Attrition	Number Surviving
Friction		
16 ICBMs	50	8
40 SLBMs	50	20
34 ALCMs	50	17
Ballistic Missile Defense		
Versus 8 ICBMs	90	1
Versus 20 SLBMs	90	2
Other defenses versus 17 ALCMs	0	17
	Total penetrating to United States	20

TABLE C.4   250 Russian Warheads (Percentages of weapons adjusted to emphasize invulnerability and cruise missiles)

Number	Type Weapon	Percent Attrition	Number Surviving
50	Mobile ICBMs	50	25
50	SLBMs at sea	50	25
50	SLBMs in port	90	5
100	ALCMs on bombers	50	50
Total 250		Total surviving U.S. attack	105

Attrition of the surviving 105 Russian Warheads
while conducting retaliatory attacks on the United States

Type Attrition	Percent Attrition	Number Surviving
Friction		
25 ICBMs	50	13
30 SLBMs	50	15
50 ALCMs	50	25
Ballistic Missile Defense		
Versus 13 ICBMs	90	1
Versus 15 SLBMs	90	2
Other defenses versus 25 ALCMs	0	25
	Total penetrating to United States	28

NOTES

Chapter One

1. Nuclear blast effects are measured in the weight of TNT that would release the same amount of energy. Because the numbers are so large, the standard measure of "yield" is in metric tonnes of TNT; to abbreviate further we talk of thousands of tonnes or kilotons (KT), or even millions of tonnes (MT). The sum of the explosive power of the 32,500 warheads in our peak inventory in 1967 was just more than 12,500 MT.

12,500 ¥ 1,000,000 tonnes/MT = 12,500,000,000 tonnes. 12,500,000,000 ¥ 2,200 lbs./tonne = 27,500,000,000,000 lbs. 27,500,000,000,000 lbs./500 lbs./bomb = 55,000,000,000 bombs.

This is not to say that 55 billion 500-pound bombs and 32,500 nuclear warheads that summed up to 12,500 MT would do identical damage; only to indicate a rough magnitude of comparison.

2. The Hiroshima bomb is estimated to have had a yield of 12.5–15.0 KT or 12,500–15,000 tonnes. The estimated total explosive power of our 32,500 warheads in 1967 was 12,500 MT or 12,500,000,000 tonnes. That total divided by 12,500 tonnes at Hiroshima is 1,000,000 Hiroshima-sized bombs.

3. Mark Selden, "The United States, Japan, and the Atomic Bomb," *Bulletin of Concerned Asian Scholars*, Vol. 23, No. 1 (January–March 1991), p. 7.

4. Richard Halloran, "Weinberger Angered by Reports on War Strategy," *New York Times*, August 24, 1982, p. B8.

5. Robert W. Tucker, "The Nuclear Debate," *Foreign Affairs* (fall 1984), p. 9.

6. Lawrence Freedman, "I Exist: Therefore I Deter," *International Security*, Vol. 13, No. 1 (summer 1988), p. 179.

7. Ibid., p. 182.

8. "Supreme Commander Pessimistic on Defense Building" (Interview with Karen Elliott House and Gerald F. Seib), *Wall Street Journal*, June 5, 1984, p. 38.

9. Author interview with Zbigniew Brzezinski, November 1996; and Robert M. Gates, *From the Shadows* (New York: Simon and Schuster, 1996), pp. 113–115.

10. Shaun Gregory, *Hidden Cost of Deterrence: Nuclear Weapons Accidents* (London: Brassey's, 1990), p. 96.

11. Melinda Lamont-Havers, *Estimated Nuclear Weapons Stockpiles, 1990–2003* (Washington, D.C.: Coalition to Reduce Nuclear Dangers, January 1997).

12. From the testimony of Dr. Bruce G. Blair, senior fellow in foreign policy studies at the Brookings Institution, before the U.S. House National Security Committee, March 13, 1997.

13. Under the NPT, the declared nuclear states (Britain, China, France, Russia, and the United States) agree not to proliferate nuclear weapons, to share benefits of peaceful nuclear technology with nonweapon states that are NPT parties, and to pursue "in good faith" negotiations to end the arms race and achieve general and complete disarmament. The nonweapon states agree not to acquire nuclear weapons or nuclear explosive devices and to submit their peaceful nuclear facilities and materials to International Atomic Energy Agency (IAEA) safeguards. Pakistan, India, and Israel are not parties to the NPT.

14. Victor A. Utgoff, *The Challenge of Chemical Weapons: An American Perspective* (New York: St. Martin's Press, 1991), p. 3.

15. Ibid., p. 4.

Chapter Two

1. The Director of Central Intelligence coordinates the twelve organizations that together make up the U.S. Intelligence Community and also heads one of those, the Central Intelligence Agency (CIA).

2. Richard P. Hallion, *Storm Over Iraq* (Washington, D.C.: Smithsonian Institution Press, 1992), p. 188.

3. U.S. Congress, Office of Technology Assessment, *The Effects of Nuclear War* (Washington, D.C.: Government Printing Office, 1979), p. 22.

4. Yuri M. Shcherbak, "Ten Years of the Chernobyl Era," *Scientific American*, April 1, 1996, pp. 44–49.

5. David A. Rosenberg, "The Origins of Overkill," *International Security*, Vol. 7, No. 4 (spring 1983), p. 55.

6. Carl von Clausewitz, *On War*, ed. and trans. Michael Howard and Peter Paret (Princeton: Princeton University Press, 1976), p. 230.

7. Fred Kaplan, *The Wizards of Armageddon* (Stanford: Stanford University Press, 1983), p. 269.

8. Alain Enthoven, as quoted in ibid., p. 254.

9. William J. Broad, "Economic Collapse Tied to Atom War," *New York Times*, June 26, 1987, p. 1.

10. Office of Technology Assessment, *The Effects of Nuclear War*, p. 21.

11. I am indebted on this point to McGeorge Bundy's excellent and thorough analysis of the Berlin crisis in his *Danger and Survival* (New York: Vintage Books, 1990), pp. 378–383.

Chapter Three

1. Carl von Clausewitz, *On War*, ed. and trans. Michael Howard and Peter Paret (Princeton: Princeton University Press, 1976), p. 67.
2. George W. Bush and Brent Scowcroft, *A World Transform*ed (New York: Knopf, 1998), p. 462–463.
3. Colin Powell with Joseph E. Persico, *My American Journey* (New York: Random House, 1995), p. 486.
4. "Assessment of the Impact of Chemical and Biological Weapons on Joint Operations in 2010 (The CB 2010 Study)," Booz Allen and Hamilton, McLean, Virginia, October 1997.

Chapter Four

1. Central Intelligence Agency, "Soviet Civil Defense," NI 78-1003, July 1978, p. 2.
2. Richard Ned Lebow, *Nuclear Crisis Management—A Dangerous Illusion* (Ithaca: Cornell University Press, 1987), p. 84.
3. McGeorge Bundy, *Danger and Survival* (New York: Vintage Books, 1990), pp. 605–606.

Chapter Five

1. I am indebted to Alton Frye for this term. See his "Banning Ballistic Missiles," *Foreign Affairs* (November/December 1996), p. 103.
2. Robin Lodge, "Russia Cannot Afford to Keep Nuclear Arsenal," *London Times*, October 7, 1998.

Chapter Six

1. This was first enunciated by the U.S. representatives at the North Atlantic Council meeting in November 1991.
2. William Drozchak, "Bonn Proposes That NATO Pledge No-First-Use of Nuclear Weapons," *Washington Post*, November 23, 1998.
3. Charles de Gaulle, "Discours et messages," cited in McGeorge Bundy, *Danger and Survival* (New York: Vintage Books, 1990), pp. 4–73.

Chapter Seven

1. Joseph Cirincione, "Why the Right Lost the Missile Defense Debate," *Foreign Policy* (spring 1997), p. 39.

2. George N. Lewis and Theodore A. Postol, "Video Evidence on the Effectiveness of Patriot During the 1991 Gulf War," *Science and Global Security*, Vol. 4. (1993), pp. 1–63.

3. R. W. Apple Jr., "Scud Missile Hits U.S. Barracks, Killing 27," *New York Times*, February 26, 1991, p. A-1.

Chapter Eight

1. "Report of the Canberra Commission on the Elimination of Nuclear Weapons," Canberra, Australia, August 1996, Executive Summary, p. 7.

2. "Troubles Invigorate Debate on START II: Russian Crisis Saps Budget for Missiles," *Washington Post*, November 19, 1998, pp. A42–43.

Chapter Nine

1. Janne Nolan, *Guardians of the Arsenal* (New York: Basic Books, 1989), p. 57.

2. Author's interview with Admiral Elmo R. Zumwalt, a member of the Joint Chiefs of Staff at that time.

3. Carl von Clausewitz, On War, ed. and trans. Michael Howard and Peter Paret (Princeton: Princeton University Press, 1976), p. 606.

Appendix A

1. U.S. Congress, Senate Foreign Relations Committee, March 1974, p. 26, cited in The Medical Implications of Nuclear War (Washington, D.C.: National Academy Press, 1986), p. 219.

2. Ibid., p. 220.

3. Kosta Tsipis, Arsenal (New York: Simon and Schuster, 1983), p. 44 (data extrapolated).

4. Richard P. Hallion, Storm over Iraq (Washington, D.C.: Smithsonian Institution Press, 1992), p. 188.

5. Theodore Postol, "Nuclear War: Effects of Nuclear Weapons," in The Encyclopedia of Americana, international ed., vol. 20 (Danbury, Conn.: Grolier, 1990), p. 519.

6. U.S. Congress, Office of Technology Assessment, The Effects of Nuclear War (Washington, D.C.: Government Printing Office, 1979), p. 16.

7. William Daugherty, Barbara Leir, and Frank von Hippel, "The Consequences of 'Limited' Nuclear Attacks on the United States," International Security, Vol. 10, No. 4 (Spring 1986), p. 19.

8. Theodore Postol, "Possible Fatalities from Superfires Following Nuclear Attacks in or Near Urban Areas," in Medical Implications of Nuclear War, p. 65.

9. Office of Technology Assessment, The Effects of Nuclear War, p. 21.

10. J. Carson Mark, The Final Epidemic (Chicago: Educational Foundation for Nuclear Science, 1981), p. 98.

11. Thesis enunciated by T. K. Jones, deputy undersecretary of defense for strategic and theater nuclear forces, as cited in Robert Scheer, With Enough Shovels (New York: Random House, 1982).

12. Daugherty, Leir, and von Hippel, "The Consequences of 'Limited' Nuclear Attacks on the United States," p. 19.

13. Steve Fetter and Kosta Tsipis, "Catastrophic Nuclear Radiation Releases," Program in Science and Technology for International Security, Report No. 5, MIT, Cambridge, Massachusetts, September 1980, p. 17.

14. Robert Ehrlich, Waging Nuclear Peace: The Technology and Politics of Nuclear Weapons (Albany: State University of New York, 1985), p. 174.

Appendix B

1. Of the extensive literature on this subject, these are the works we referred to most: S. Glasstone and P. Dolan, eds., The Effects of Nuclear Weapons, Government Printing Office, 1977; Congressional Office of Technology Assessment (OTA), The Effects of Nuclear War, Government Printing Office, 1979; Arms Control and Disarmament Agency (ACDA), An Analysis of Civil Defense in Nuclear War, 1978; W. Daugherty, B. Levi, and F. von Hippel, "The Consequences of 'Limited' Nuclear Attacks on the United States," International Security, Spring, 1986; T. Postol, Possible Fatalities from Superfires Following Nuclear Attacks in or Near Urban Areas, paper presented at the Institute of Medicine's Symposium on the Medical Effects of Nuclear War, National Academy of Sciences, Washington, D.C., September 20–22, 1985; AMBIO, Nuclear War: The Aftermath, Volume XI, Number 2–3, 1985; A. M. Katz, Life After Nuclear War, Ballinger, 1982; R. Goen, R. Bothun, and F. Walker, Potential Vulnerability Affecting National Survival (PVANS), Stanford Research Institute (SRI), September 1970; F. Dresch and S. Baum, Analysis of the U.S. and USSR Potential for Economic Recovery Following A Nuclear Attack, Stanford Research Institute, 1973; Economic Model commissioned by Federal Emergency Management Agency as described in Development of a Dynamic Model to Evaluate Economic Recovery Following a Nuclear Attack, Final Report, Volume I: Description and Simulations, November 1980, Pugh-Roberts Associates, Inc., Cambridge, MA.

2. Water Resources Support Center, U.S. Corps of Engineers, Port Series, Government Printing Office, 1983–84.

3. Assistant Secretary for Fossil Energy, Department of Energy, Strategic Petroleum Reserve: Annual Report, Government Printing Office, 1984. R.G. Lawson, "Strategic Petroleum Construction Ends First Phase," Oil and Gas Journal, 21 July 1980.

4. Aileen Cantrell, "Annual Refining Survey," Oil and Gas Journal, March 1983, 1984, and 1985.

5. Penn Well Maps, Product Pipelines of the United States and Canada, Penn Well Publishing, 1983; Crude Oil Pipelines of the United States and Canada, Penn Well Publishing, 1982; Natural Gas Pipelines of the United States and Canada, Penn Well Publishing, 1982.

6. As discussed previously, this happened to some extent in both Japan and Germany after World War II.

7. Imports cannot be relied on forever. If imports become an external crutch for the U.S. economy, then the internal rebuilding process can be slowed down, which can seriously hurt the long-term prospects for the economy.

8. As we have said before, if the point of the attack is to collapse the U.S. economy and keep it from recovering, the Soviets might well target a few weapons on Canada and Mexico to put them in no position to aid the United States, at least in the short term when it is the most critical.

INDEX

Gross domestic product (GDP), 91
Gross national product (GNP), 39, 160,
    166, 167
Groundbursts, 35, 154
Gulf War, 4, 54, 55, 56–57, 76, 101, 103
    and civil defense, 106

Hague Conventions, 25
Hamas, 28
Health. *See* Medical issues
Health and Human Services Department,
    110
Hiroshima, 1, 2, 9, 12, 34
Horner, Charles, 142–143
House of Representatives, 31
Hungary, 102
Hussein, Saddam, 27, 56, 76. *See also* Gulf
    War; Iraq
Hypocrisy, 11, 12

ICBMs. *See* Intercontinental ballistic
    missiles
Iceland, 132
Immigration and Naturalization Service,
    110
Immunizations, 106–107
Impediments to strategic escrow process,
    85–86
Imports, 164(fig.)
India, 19, 20, 23, 68, 69, 94, 123
Information to citizens, 145–146
Inoculations, 106–107
Insects,
Intelligence issues. *See* Central Intelligence
    Agency (CIA)
Interagency coordination, 109–112
Intercontinental ballistic missiles (ICBMs),
    8, 15–16, 17(table), 31, 53, 70
    Iran, 99
    Korea, 99
    See also Defenses
International Criminal Court, 121
International intelligence sharing, 124
International Science and Technology
    Center (ISTC), 126
Iran, 1, 23, 77, 117

and intercontinental ballistic missiles,
    99
Iraq, 1, 4, 20, 21, 23, 61, 77
    and nuclear capability, 99, 117
    and United Nations, 28, 117–118, 120,
    123–124
    See also Gulf War
Israel, 19, 20, 23, 68, 94, 103, 106, 123
ISTC. *See* International Science and
    Technology Center
Italy, 25, 89

Japan, 25–26, 27, 58, 93, 103, 126
Joint Chiefs of Staff, 133, 138
Joint Committee on Atomic Energy, 139,
    140
Jungle warfare, 68
Justice Department, 110, 113

Kaffa, 24
Kazakhstan, 21, 87, 126
Keeley, John B., 89–90
Kennedy, John, 44, 65, 134
Khrushchev, Nikita, 44
Kilotons (KT), 33–34, 46, 149, 158
Kirkuk, 76
Kissinger, Henry, 14, 91
Korean War, 26
KT. *See* Kilotons
Kurds, 27, 64
Kuwait, 57, 61. *See also* Gulf War

Launch on warning, 16
LeMay, Curtis, 133, 135, 143, 144
Lethality of nuclear weapons/warheads,
    44–45, 145, 149–158
Libya, 120
Liquid fuel systems, 39–40. *See also*
    Transportation
Lisbon, 12
Lobbying, 10
Lugar, Richard, 109, 125

McNamara, Robert S., 13, 133, 142
Maginot Line, 97
Manhattan Project, 144